Multi-Track Modular Teaching

An Advanced Teaching-Learning Method

B. S. Manoj

June 2019.

Library of Congress Cataloguing-in-Publication Data:

B. S. Manoj

Multi-Track Modular Teaching: An Advanced Teaching-Learning Method

ISBN-13: 978-93-5361-582-6 (International Paperback Edition)

1. Teaching 2. Multi-modal learning 3. Higher education 4. Undergraduate research

Paperback Book prepared in Trivandrum, India.
Published by B. S. Manoj (imprint ***bsmp***)
Sree, ANRA-E-5/2, C. S. Nagar Road, Trivandrum, 695587, India.

This book is the first in the Mentoring Series by Dr. B. S. Manoj

Cover Design by Dr. B. S. Manoj
Editing by Dr. B. S. Manoj
Manuscript Review by Er. Sarath Babu
Cover design review by Dr. Swapna U. P.
Forewords by **Dr. B. N. Suresh and Dr. V. K. Dadhwal**

June 2019

Multi-Track Modular Teaching

An Advanced Teaching-Learning Method

B. S. Manoj

Tags: Non-fiction, Higher education, Teaching, Multi-modal teaching-learning, Undergraduate research

Book Description

Multi-Track Modular Teaching is an Advanced Teaching-Learning method for higher education that utilizes various tracks within an academic course. MT2 method effectively enables multi-modal learning for students. Contents of the tracks are designed with modularity for better handling. How to design the tracks? How many tracks are most suited? What are the example tracks one can use? How to design the modularity of tracks? How many modules are most suited? All these questions are answered in this book. MT2 method is developed at the Indian Institute of Space science and Technology over the last eight years by an expert academician. MT2 method can be utilized by universities for courses where deeper learning is essential.

Brief About the Author

B. S. Manoj is Professor and Head of Avionics Department of Indian Institute of Space science and Technology (IIST), Trivandrum, India. Prior to joining IIST, he was with University of California San Diego, San Diego, CA, USA. His research interests are in Computer Networks, Complex Networks, Wireless Networks, Ad Hoc Wireless Networks, Cyber Security, Satellite Networks, and Next Generation Internet.

Dedication

This book is dedicated to

Prof. C. Siva Ram Murthy, PhD,
My PhD advisor and Richard Karp Institute Chair Professor at the Indian Institute of Technology Madras (IITM), Chennai, India.

Prof. Ramesh Rao, PhD, and
My Post-Doctoral Advisor and Qualcomm Endowed Chair Professor at the University of California San Diego, CA 92093, USA.

Prof. V. Prithiviraj, PhD.
My MTech Advisor and Principal (Retd.), Pondicherry Engineering College, Pondicherry, India.

Table of Contents

Foreword

Indian Institute of Space science and Technology (IIST), Trivandrum, established by Department of Space has been focusing on the advanced areas of research related to space science and technology right from the beginning. The Institute has also been introducing many technology innovations, which also include a new teaching method, Multi-Track Modular Teaching (MT2). This in my opinion is indeed a novel method for the conduct of advanced academic classes.

The MT2 method has been captured nicely in this book and I am quite happy to go through the manuscripts and at the same time found it quite interesting. No doubt, it provides a fulcrum for teaching in senior UG and Masters classes which can be effectively used to enhance deeper and all-round learning of a subject. The proposed method defines a pedagogical structure for class room interaction, between a teacher and students, by defining multiple tracks with each track consisting of a series of modules. By careful selection of tracks and the modules, a teacher can create the needed depth in several directions in a research-oriented teaching class.

The MT2 method developed by Dr. B. S. Manoj, an excellent teacher at IIST, is refined over several years by adopting the practices suggested in the book, in the elective courses of computer networks. One important aspect about MT2 method is its suitability for enhancing UG research in universities. Encouraging research at the young UG ages helps the brilliant students to take on further research. IIST has been pioneering the UG research from the beginning and I am happy to see that the MT2 has been effectively implemented in the elective courses in order to inculcate the research activities amongst the students.

I am very confident that the readers of this book would greatly benefit in having a lucid understanding of the proposed MT2 method. I also recommend to teachers, and academic administrators to consider adopting the proposed teaching method which would vastly help to enhance the quality of teaching and also the culture of research.

I take this opportunity to convey my very best to all readers.

Dr. B. N. Suresh
Chancellor, IIST Trivandrum, 695547, India.

Foreword

Developments of teaching-learning processes have been of critical importance in the evolution of mankind. Ancient India was known for traditional knowledge and wisdom in many areas of art, science, technology, and medicine and a unique guru-shishya culture for teaching-learning had evolved. The focus on education and teaching continues.

I am very happy that a new academic course organization method, Multi-Track Modular Teaching (MT2), has emerged and been adopted in the class rooms of the Indian Institute of Space science and Technology (IIST), Trivandrum, India. As you may be aware, IIST is the first university, in India, focusing on space science and technology and working closely with the Indian Space Research Organization (ISRO). IIST encourages development of not only new knowledge on space science and technology, but also education and training techniques to accomplish this task.

This MT2 method provides students with multi-faceted learning about a subject. The key aspect I found in MT2 method is the multi-modality of tracks that enable different facets of learning. I also find the MT2 approach is simple to adopt in today's curricula. The method brings in benefits of laboratory as well as real-world learning in academic courses. MT2 offers a unique way of introducing experimental and other support components in a flexible and adaptive manner to complement the lectures in an academic course.

I have high confidence that the readers will immensely benefit from this book.

Dr. Vinay Kumar Dadhwal
Director
Indian Institute of Space science and Technology

Trivandrum, 695547, India.
Email: vkdadhwal@iist.ac.in, dadhwalvk@hotmail.com
https://www.linkedin.com/in/vinaykdadhwal/

Preface

Effective teaching is a challenging process. A teaching process is useful when it helps in imparting knowledge to a student community. Given the time and resources both the teachers and students dedicate for the teaching-learning process, it is important to identify, develop, and practice more effective teaching methods. This book proposes a new advanced teaching method called Multi-Track Modular Teaching (MT2) method, developed at the Indian Institute of Space science and Technology (IIST), Trivandrum, India. MT2 method helps in all-round and deeper learning about a particular academic subject or trade area.

MT2 method suggests organizing an academic course into multiple tracks alongside the main lecture track. Each of these tracks is further divided into modules for better handling the topics covered in a course. The tracks cover learning activities that complement the main lecture track. MT2 method is a good tool for enabling undergraduate research in universities.

This book provides a detailed description of how an instructor can utilize MT2 method in a university system. It also describes many examples for the design of tracks and modules for various academic and trade areas. Practical examples from my long-standing academic courses at IIST have been included in this book.

I would like to express my sincere gratitude to my mentors Prof. C. Siva Ram Murthy, Prof. Ramesh Rao, and Prof. V. Prithiviraj, for the training I received under them over the years. Their influence has driven me in words, deeds, and thoughts, to make me what I am today. No amount of words can be enough to thank a teacher who made a difference to an individual.

I would like to express my sincere gratitude to Dr. B. N. Suresh, Chancellor, Indian Institute of Space science and Technology (IIST), Thiruvananthapuram, India for his mentoring. I thank Dr. Vinay Kumar Dadhwal, Director, IIST, for his constant encouragement and permission to publish this book. My thanks are extended to Dr. Y. V. N. Krishnamurthy, Senior Professor and Registrar, IIST. Further, I would like to thank Prof. Joseph Kuruvilla, Prof. Raju George, Prof. Kurien Issac,

Prof. A. Chandrasekhar, and Prof. Narayana Murthy, for various helps during my work at IIST.

Further, I would like to express my sincere gratitude to my collaborators Prof. Bheemarjuna Reddy Tamma and Prof. Venkata Ramana Badarla.

I also express my thanks to Indian Institute of Space science and Technology (IIST) faculty members Prof. Deepak Mishra and Prof. B. S. Vineeth. My PhD students Sarath Babu, Abhishek Chakraborty, Debabrata Dalai, and Avinash Chalumuri had helped me in various ways during the preparation of the course work that I taught using MT2 method at IIST. I would like to thank them for their support.

Many of my former undergraduate students who undertook some of my courses where I practiced MT2 method helped me revise, refine, and improve the format of MT2-based courses. Some of them continue to interact with me well after their graduation including, but not limited to, Mr. Nitish Kumar, Ms. Nivedita Gaur, Ms. Ishita Ganjoo, Mr. Gaurav Jain, Ms. Priti Singh, Ms. Pragya Shah, and Ms. Archana C. M.

I also would like to thank Dr. Gadepalli Venkata Viswanath Sharma, Dr. Veeramani Mahendran, Mr. Najeem M. S. Hameed, Dr. Sreejith V. Nair, and Dr. Deepthi Chander, who, during their student days, underwent the summer training program at University of California San Diego (UCSD) division of CalIT2, in summer 2009 as part of program titled *Indo-US Advanced Summer School on Systems and Networks*. Further, I express my thanks to Prof. S. Dharmaraja, Prof. U. B. Desai, Prof. Geoff Voelker, Prof. George Varghese, Prof. Krishna Sivalingam, Prof. S. N. Merchant, Prof. Rajesh Gupta, Prof. Bhaskar Rao, Dr. Dilip Krishnaswamy, Dr. Navid Ehsan, Dr. Ping Zhou, Dr. Kalyan Vaidyanathan, Dr. Sameer Tilak, Dr. Anders Nilsson Plymoth, Mr. Srinivas Sukumar, and Ms. Lovella Cacho, who helped conduct the summer school program at UCSD.

Ms. Preetha S and Mr. Vijaya Kumar Nair, Members of Office staff, Department of Avionics, IIST and Ms. Divya R. S., lab tutor at Systems and Networks Lab, IIST, helped in many logistics arrangements during the preparation of this book. Similarly, I thank the IIST library staff, particularly our librarian Mr. Abdunnasar A, and staff of the reprographic section of IIST library for various kinds of helps during the preparation of the book.

I express my gratitude to my parents Shri. K. Balakrishnan Nair and G. Santhakumari Amma, my brothers Dr. Bindukumar Nair and Advocate B. S. Harikrishnan, my Wife Dr. Swapna U.P., my daughter Gouri Nair, and my friends and colleagues who stood by me during the preparation of the book. I thank all of them for accepting my absence from their life during the preparation of this book. I also thank my office conveyance colleagues, Prof. Sam Zachariah and Prof. Anup S, for their support and encouragement.

I would like to thank Honorable Minister Shri. Prakash Javadekar, served during 2014-2019 at the Ministry of Human Resource Development, Government of India and all officials of MHRD who helped organize the Pandit Madan Mohan Malavia National Program on Teachers and Teaching (PMMMNPTT). Further, I extend my gratitude to Prof. G. Mohan and all his staff at Administrative Staff College, Hyderabad India, for coordinating the Innovative Teacher Award Program 2016 under the Pandit Madan Mohan Malavya National Program on Teachers and Teaching. MT2 method was recognized as one of the 15 teaching Innovations under the above mentioned program organized by MHRD, Government of India. I appreciate and thank my co-winners of the MHRD sponsored Innovative Teacher 2016 program. An image of the certificate/award is provided in the author's biography at the end of this book.

I have made good amount of care to avoid any typographical errors. However, if you spot any errors or omissions, kindly let me know so that future editions of this book can be produced without them.

I sincerely hope this book will benefit you.

B. S. Manoj
Emails: bsmanoj@ieee.org, bsmanoj@gmail.com
Web: https://www.iist.ac.in/avionics/bsmanoj
https://iist-sysnet.github.io/

Chapter 1
Introduction

Tell me and I forget;
Show me and I remember;
Involve me and I understand.
- Chinese proverb.

1.1 The Genesis

The genesis of the multi-track modular teaching method goes back to 2009 when I was working as an Assistant Research Scientist and Lecturer at the California Institute of Telecommunications and Information Technology[1] (CalIT2) of University of California San Diego (UCSD), La Jolla, San Diego, USA. I had then received a grant for conducting a summer school titled Indo-US Advanced Summer School on Systems and Networks [19][2] from Indo-US Science and Technology Forum (IUSSTF) [18] during 18th June 2009 to 18th July 2009. Prof. S. Dharmaraja [7], Department of Mathematics, Indian Institute of Technology Delhi (IITD), New Delhi, India was the co-principal investigator of the summer school. As part of the summer school, we invited a few selected students, for a month-long training program, from various premier Indian institutions. The selected students were from Indian Institute of Technology Madras (IITM), Chennai, India and Indian Institute of Technology Bombay (IITB), Mumbai, India. Prof. Ramesh Rao, my post-doctoral research advisor, who directed the UCSD Division of CalIT2 at that time, encouraged us to think very creatively and prepare a novel training program. In our research group, CalIT2 Systems and Networks research group (CalSysNet) [4], we came up with a training program with multiple series (or tracks) of activities for the participating students. As per one of the series (tracks), we created a Lecture track where I delivered a series of technical lectures on distributed wireless networks. Another track consisted of lectures by eminent professors from UCSD, Indian Institutions of Technology (IITs), and other US organizations. A third track focused on hands-on training of advanced wireless network prototypes such as building wireless mesh network routers and cognitive network prototypes. The hands-on training track was chaired by my then colleague Dr. Bheemarjuna Reddy Tamma [8]. The summer school turned out to be a grand success. During the review of the overall event, I noticed that the multiple diverse tracks we used in the training program has been the principal factor that made the training program very effective, particularly on imparting an all-round learning experience for the participating students. In January 2011, I returned to India and accepted a faculty position at the Indian Institute of Space science and Technology (IIST) [17], Trivandrum, India. I decided to introduce a senior undergraduate elective course on Wireless Mesh Networks (WMN) in a novel manner using the parallel track approach. I refined and improved the structure of the Indo-US Summer school program in order to suit a semester-long academic course of 3-4 credits. The result was the multi-track modular teaching method. In July-December 2011 semester, I offered a new elective course (AV 484 Wireless Mesh Networks) that used the multi-track modular teaching method with three tracks for the first time. At the end of the course, I found that my students benefitted substantially from the course. Many students were surprised by the depth of learning they had experienced. My faculty evaluation feedback soared to EXCELLENT. Further, many graduated students wanted me to offer similar multi-tracked teaching method to the subsequent years too. In the subsequent years, I improved the course with richer tracks resulting in the current level that I follow in my current courses where I use utmost four tracks with contents of the tracks varying each year. Thus born, the idea of the Multi-Track Modular Teaching (MT2) method!

1.2 Why I Wrote this Book?

In 2016, Ministry of Human Resources Development (MHRD) of Government of India called for recognizing innovative teaching methodologies developed in India. When I approached Dr. Vinay Kumar Dadhwal [9], Director, IIST, he encouraged and recommended to make an application based on MT2 method. MHRD short-listed MT2 method as one of the innovations and asked me clarifications on how it can be utilized for various situations. I promptly responded with examples and details. They came back again and wanted me to give more clarifications. Once again, I supplied them with detailed and satisfactory explanation. As a result of a series of evaluations, clarifications, and short-listing, they identified and short-listed MT2 method as one of the 15 innovative teaching techniques from a large number of, more than 200, novel teaching-learning tools, techniques, or methods in late 2016. The innovators whose ideas were short-listed were asked to present before a high level committee headed by Prof. G. Mohan, Professor and Director, Centre for Innovation and Technology, Administrative Staff College of India (ASCI), Hyderabad, India [2]. After the presentation and evaluation, I received a congratulatory call from Prof. G. Mohan and he sent me commendation note based on their evaluation. Subsequently, in 2019, I was invited to attend a function organized by the MHRD where the then Cabinet Minister of Government of India, Shri. Prakash Javadekar handed over to me a certificate in honor of my teaching innovation. An image of the certificate is shown in the Author's biography at the end of this book. During my presentations to the MHRD committee, they suggested me to create a document about the concept of MT2 method for the wider distribution and use of the academic, research, and training community. This book is a result of the encouragement received from them. I believe this book will help a large number of higher education institutions around the world on improving the teaching-learning process using MT2 method.

1.3 Why MT2 Method?

In many academic institutions, students may not benefit from the courses even after spending a full semester with an academic course. As a result, their expected expertise in the subject is under-accomplished and students' employability is severely affected. With inadequate learning, the graduates become a burden in all spheres of the society. It is in the best interest of the society, we need to create and utilize effective learning strategies.

When I started teaching at IIST, I decided to introduce the new teaching method that can make students learn several research-related aspect of the subject. Many of my own dissertation-students were lacking the essential skills in the area of dissertation when they joined me. As a response, I used the Multi-Track Modular Teaching (MT2) method. My main purpose in introducing the method is to get the undergraduate students trained to do research. Unlike other undergraduate students, the students who are accepted to do their dissertation work in my lab, spanning the entire last semester of their UG curriculum, required a level of additional knowledge so that they will be productive to do their research-oriented dissertation work. I encouraged students to do research by including certain amount of undergraduate research activities as part of their undergraduate courses. My use of MT2 method benefitted the students significantly in doing successful dissertation work. In the following section, I discuss the key benefits of MT2 method.

1.3.1 Key Benefits of MT2 Method

MT2 method formalizes a structure for multi-modal teaching possibilities such that teachers in universities can achieve many benefits. Some of these benefits are briefly presented here:

- Enhanced quality of teaching
- Enhanced students' engagement with the subject
- Deeper and better understanding of the subject
- Enhanced students' confidence
- Removal of students' fear factor
- Improved employability of students
- Training students to carry out special education such as research

1.3.2 How MT2 Method is Useful for UG Research?

World's best universities excel in Undergraduate research (UG research). UG research is the foundation of high quality scientists, researchers, and the success behind the establishment of knowledge-based economy. Most US universities have large UG population, however, only a small part of them undertake UG research. Even such a small fraction of UG researchers do eventually become great scientists and engineers. Europe has a bigger fraction of UG students undertaking research related activities than the USA. In India, one of the best examples for UG research is the Indian Institute of Space science and Technology (IIST), Trivandrum, India. The prestigious Indian Institutes of Technology (IITs) have also advanced the concept of UG research. MT2 method provides a foundation for enabling effective UG research in any university that aspires to excel and develop as a modern university of our generation. Chapter 5 provides a detailed discussion on the possibility of using MT2 at various levels of UG research.

1.3.3 The Impact of MT2 Method

I have practiced MT2 method for regular class room use over the last eight years of my service at IIST Trivandrum, India. Most of my uses of MT2 are for senior elective courses for undergraduate students where student strength varied between 20 to 45 students. I also had used MT2 for core courses with upto sixty students. The method is refined over the years to what is presented in this book.

The major observations I made on the dimensions of the impact of MT2 can be summarized as follows: (i) better learning outcome due to multi-modal teaching, (ii) better writing ability, (iii) better research skills, (iv) better teacher-student relationship, and (v) better employability of students.

I have observed substantial improvement in learning outcome of the students whenever I utilized MT2 in my courses. The main benefit came due to the multi-modality of learning directions. Due to the multi-modality of learning, students are better engaged in the courses, thus resulting in enhanced learning.

I also observed students developing better technical writing skills by the courses where there were tracks on writing or preparing write-ups. In fact, I noticed that many students who undertook an MT2-based course wrote better final undergraduate dissertation work. Several undergraduate students published research papers during the elective courses as a result of their learning on the theoretical, practical, and writing skills.

Among the students who have carried out their final Undergraduate dissertation work under my guidance, those who undertook an MT2-based course clearly outperformed with much better research output. In fact, one of the reasons of my development of MT2 method was to train undergraduate students to do better research.

More importantly, I found that the relationship between the students and the teacher is rather strong when a course is conducted based on MT2 method. One of the reasons for a strengthened bond between the teacher and students is the collective effort in working out some of the tracks of the course, particularly the experimental tracks. That is, in courses where there is a prototype network testbed planned for design, development, and deployment, the working relationship between the teachers, teaching assistants, and students have become very friendly and strong.

Finally, those students who undertook courses under MT2 method have been found to be better prepared for employment. Some of my students have been placed on suitable employments as soon as they started applying for jobs. Multi-modality brings out better learning as well as confidence for students, thus resulting in their better prospects for employability.

1.4 When to Use MT2 Method?

A few situations where we can immensely benefit from practicing MT2 method are as follows:

- When you teach an academic course for a set of students who will be required to do a dissertation/thesis work in the area of the course.
- When you teach a specialized course that requires significant practical/hands-on content.
- When you teach a course that is expected to provide a very deep level of knowledge in the course topics.
- When you teach a course that has student strength, preferably, in the range of 40-60 students.
- When you teach a course that is expected to produce students with substantial research skills on the topic.

1.5 When Not to Use MT2 Method?

While MT2 method is very effective for deeper learning as well as better teaching-learning process, it may not be the right choice in certain situations. A few situations where MT2 method may not be beneficial are listed as follows: (i) General/Basic courses, (ii) Very large and unscalable classes, (iii) Depth-less courses, (iv) Faculty with insufficient expertise, and (v) Faculty with resource constraints.

1.5.1 General/Basic Courses

When you teach a general or basic course that provides only a high-level or introductory knowledge about a topic, MT2 method is not essential. There exist many academic as well as non-academic courses where depth may not be expected. For example, a general introductory course at an undergraduate level or high school level may not require highly focused training in a specialized area. In fact, introducing MT2 method in its true form may prove counter-productive when used for basic or introductory courses. In such courses, deeper learning can result in specialization that may not be essential.

1.5.2 Very Large and Unscalable Classes

When you teach a large class without sufficient number of teaching assistants or teaching assistants without sufficient expertise, then the effective practice of MT2 method may not be feasible to its intended level. Therefore, in such cases, MT2 method may be avoided because attempting to use MT2 method can result in low levels of students' satisfaction leading to unsatisfactory feedback from students. Unsatisfactory student feedback may affect the confidence of even experienced faculty whereas it may cost the employment of junior or contract faculty. While using MT2 is challenging for very large physical classes, Massive Open Online Courses (MOOCs) can utilize MT2 very effectively, as discussed later in this chapter.

1.5.3 Depth-less Courses

When you teach a course that covers a broader topic without sufficient depth, MT2 method need not be required. Multi-modal teaching methods such as MT2 method is most useful when deeper learning and depth of teaching are required.

1.5.4 Faculty with Insufficient Expertise

When a teacher does not have sufficient expertise in the area of the course he/she teaches, introducing MT2 method will help only the teacher, not the students. While an attempt in using MT2 method may improve the knowledge level of the teacher in the area of the course, it is not advised because that does not benefit the students who are the intended recipients of the course.

1.5.5 Faculty Resource Constraints

Time is a very important ingredient needed for conducting an academic course using MT2 method. When an instructor teaches a course that otherwise meets all the requirements of MT2 method, it need not be considered for MT2 method if the instructor does not have sufficient time to invest in teaching the course. If the instructor cannot dedicate sufficient time, MT2 method may not be effective.

1.6 How to Use MT2 Method for MOOCs?

Massive Open Online Courses (MOOCs) are new generation web-based class rooms that offer the most transforming classroom approaches in the teaching-learning environment. The spread of Internet and Web-based technologies provide the foundation of the MOOC system. Many classes conducted by the leading MOOC providers, Udacity [33], EdX [11], and Coursera [6], have found very large number of students in the enrollment of some of the courses. Similarly, the National Program on Technology Enhanced Learning (NPTEL) program

[23] of Indian Institutions of Technologies (IITs) and Swayam [31] Program of the Ministry of Human Resource Development of India, are examples of massive online learning platforms.

Since MT2 method is a concept where the traditional teaching process in a course is converted into a multi-modal teaching process by using multiple tracks, adopting MT2 to MOOCs is easy and effective. In a MOOC course, the activity tracks can be easily planned and executed. Tracks can be defined during the early stage of introducing the course and activity modules can be scheduled for each track. Without revealing the surprise elements of the modules of the tracks, the modules can be introduced to the students through the online system. In most MOOC systems, the evaluation is also done through automated software systems. Therefore, most of the modules can also be evaluated through the online system. However, MOOC introduces certain limitations in utilizing the capability of tracks that involve creative work. For example, if a particular course that is following MT2 method conducts a Creative Writing Track or experimental work with real-systems, then the students' submissions cannot be evaluated through ordinary software systems. Therefore, except the tracks that require high creativity to answer the questions or when real-world experiments are not involved, MOOC system can utilize MT2 method very effectively.

1.7 Organization of the Book

The organization of the book is as follows.

This introductory chapter briefly presented the genesis, motivation as well as when to use and when not to use MT2 method. The Chapter 2 provides details of MT2 method, various example formats, as well as highlighting some benefits.

Chapter 3 provides information on the tracks and how to design the tracks for an MT2 method-based course. The types of tracks are critical in the effective conduct of MT2 method. The chapter also highlights the merits and demerits of the courses with large number of tracks.

Chapter 4 focuses on the modularity of the tracks. How to design modularity, what types of modules can be effective, and how to determine the types of modularity, and their pros and cons are discussed.

In Chapter 5, a specific set of thoughts is provided on how MT2 method can be utilized for enabling undergraduate research. Further, the credit distribution as well as focused use of MT2 method for research oriented courses is presented.

Chapter 6 presents glimpses of various teaching philosophies from around the world. Further, a few productivity enhancement tools, useful to teachers and students, such as Cornell note-taking method, Franklin's chart, Eisenhower's matrix, and the Three Bins technique are also discussed.

Chapter 7 concludes the book.

1.8 Summary

This chapter discussed the genesis of MT2 method and brief discussion on the definition of the method. Further, the chapter presented when to use and when not to use MT2 method. The chapter concluded by briefly discussing the organization of the rest of the book.

Acquire new knowledge whilst thinking over the old, and you may become a teacher of others.

- Confucius.

Chapter 2
The Method

The function of education is to teach one to think intensively and to think critically. Intelligence plus character - that is the goal of true education.
- Martin Luther King, Jr.

2.1 In Simple Words

In simple words, Multi-Track Modular Teaching (MT2) method is an innovative teaching methodology where an academic course is divided into multiple parallel tracks where each track consists of a modular set of activities that collectively provide a deeper learning about the topic under study. The tracks are organized as one main track and other tracks complementing the main track. Each track focuses on distinct and specific set of topics/activities. Each track is organized as clearly defined modules that accomplish the objectives of the track. MT2 method enhances the students' interest, engagement, and learning level. MT2 method can be easily introduced in today's university-driven academic curriculum all around the world.

2.2 The Method in Detail

Course organization in most universities is determined and implemented by the instructors based on an approved curriculum and syllabi. The curriculum and syllabi are usually prepared after wider consultation within the university with internal and external academic experts before finally approved by Board of Studies, Academic Council, Senate, or equivalent bodies. Instructors usually dedicate themselves in delivering the lectures to the best they can. They also try to bring in novelty in teaching by trying out variations in style of teaching, introducing special assignments, as well as even conducting some of the class-room experiments. Every teacher has a unique style of instruction. Great teachers such as Professor Walter Lewin of Massachusetts Institute of Technology (MIT), whose Physics lectures were most sought after lectures during his service at MIT, had developed his own unique styles. Professor Walter Lewin dedicated himself for his lectures by conducting physics experiments in front of large number of students in the class. Some of the experiments involved special setup including large physical apparatus, timers, and various instruments to prove scientific principles in the class. In one of his famous classroom experiments, he himself sat on a gigantic pendulum to prove the equation corresponding to the frequency, wavelength, and independence of the mass and period of the pendulum. Such introduction of novelty in classroom teaching style is one of the key aspects that differentiate great teachers.

MT2 method organizes an academic course into a small number of distinct tracks. The first track is defined as the main track. Usually, the main track is a Lecture track where the class-room or video lectures are delivered to students by following the syllabus of the course. The tracks other than the main track support the main track in meeting the objectives of the course. That is, the main track, usually a lectures track, is supported by the rest of the tracks in a complementary manner. Each of these support tracks complements the other tracks with minimal overlap among themselves. The purpose of each track shall be clearly defined and communicated to the students in the early stages of the course. The selection and contents of the track can be defined and implemented by the instructor. An instructor can define the contents as per his/her plan and decision to enhance the teaching-learning process as well as to meet the objectives of the course. It is possible that some tracks can be bigger than the others. Appropriate credit distribution can be made among the tracks to evaluate and grade the students. The number of tracks within a course shall be limited to bare-minimal and in most 3-credit semester-long courses, 3-4 tracks can be most appropriate.

Track-1: Lecture	Track-2: Design and Development	Track-3: Documentation	Track-4: Review
Intro to spacecraft design	Mission Identification and analysis		
Subsystem Design	Preliminary Design	Mission design document	
System Architecture Design	Design of Subsystems	Preliminary Design Document	Mission Review
Integrated System Design	Detailed Design of the System	Detailed Design of Subsystems	Preliminary Design Review
Qualification and Checkout Process	System integration	Detailed Integrated System Design Document	Detailed Design Review
	Checkout and Qualification	System integration and Qualification Document	Final Review

Figure 2.1: An Example of Tracks and Modules for a Hypothetical Spacecraft Design and Development Course using MT2 Method.

Figure 2.1 illustrates a four track hypothetical course on *Spacecraft Design and Development* as an example to illustrate MT2 method. A spacecraft is a device, machine, or vehicle with or without human crew inside, to fly in a controlled manner in lower atmosphere, outer atmosphere, or deep space environment. A spacecraft usually is controlled by human beings from a command and control station located at ground stations on earth. Satellites of various kinds, such as those used for remote sensing, communications, navigation, and military purposes, are examples of spacecrafts. Universities can use MT2 method where spacecrafts can be designed as part of the courses by the students. The four tracks shown in Figure 2.1 are the following: (i) Track-1: Lecture track, (ii) Track-2: Design and Development track, (iii) Track-3: Documentation track, and (iv) Track-4: Review track.

The main track is Track-1 (Lecture track) that covers the classroom lectures on spacecraft design. In this track, the instructor is expected to lecture the students on various elements of spacecraft design. The Lecture track can be modularly organized for the convenience of teaching. The main modules of the Track-1 are as follows: (i) Introduction to spacecraft design, (ii) Subsystem design, (iii) System architecture design, (iv) Integrated system design, and (v) Qualification process. The Track-1 modules are typically defined based on the contents of the course syllabus. The rest of the tracks support the main track towards developing students for meeting the objectives of the course.

Track-2 (Design and Development track) covers the modules for the process of spacecraft design. The modularity of the Spacecraft Design and Development track can help in reducing the complexity of spacecraft design by the subsystems designs as well as the integration of various subsystem designs in order to meet the final objective of the spacecraft design. The Track-2 has the following modules: (i) Mission identification and analysis, (ii) Preliminary design, (iii) Detailed design of the system, (iv) System integration, and (v) Check out and qualification. Since Track-2 in this case is quite intensive, sufficient credit/mark shall be assigned to reward the students or student teams based on their progress.

The Track-3 is Documentation track that deals with the students producing satisfactory documentation for their designs carried out as part of the Track-2. In many projects, the creation of documentation is not given sufficient attention, while documentation is as important as design or development is. In order to identify the importance of documentation as equal to the design activity, the definition of a separate Documentation track greatly helps. The major modules in this track are as follows: (i) Mission design document, (ii) Preliminary design document, (iii) Detailed design of subsystems, (iv) Detailed integrated system design document, (v) System integration and qualification document.

Finally, the Track-4 deals with the review sequence. In most satellite or space mission projects, there exists a series of reviews such as Preliminary Design Reviews (PDRs), Detailed Technical Reviews (DTRs), Mission Readiness Reviews (MRRs), in addition to the periodic progress reviews at various levels. In a class, focusing on spacecrafts' development, the key elements of the reviews shall be included. In the example course, shown in Figure 2.1, the major modules of Track-4 include the following: (i) Mission review, (ii) Preliminary design review, (iii) Detailed design review, and (iv)

Final review. In fact, the identification of reviews as a separate track help in communicating the importance of the reviews to the students.

Each of the tracks in a course that follows MT2 method, is divided into a set of adaptive and customizable modules as discussed above. The organizations of tracks into modules help better deliver the track's contents as well as help simplify the evaluation process. The modules within a track are adaptive and customizable in the sense that as the course proceeds, the contents of the modules can be suitably modified. Some of the modules can also offer challenging activities. The difficulty levels of modules in a track can be organized such that there is progressive change in the difficulty levels. During the progress of a course, the instructor may modify or customize the modules based on the feedback and ability of students to undertake the tasks.

Example of Tracks in IIST AV 484 course in 2012

Track-1: Lectures	Track-2: Seminar Track	Track-3: WMN Testbed
Attend the lectures (80% attendance required)	Review 3-4 research papers from IEEE/ACM/Elsevier digital libraries	Form teams and learn how to develop a WMN router
Write Quizzes (Two)	Prepare a seminar presentation based on the papers	Learn how to install routing and other protocols in your router
Write Final Exams (One)	Revise it sufficiently well to improve the quality of writeup (No plagiarism)	Learn how to build a network testbed
Get sufficient points	Present the Seminar in the class.	Deploy the network testbed in IIST campus.

Figure 2.2: MT2 Example for AV 484 Wireless Mesh Networks 2012 conducted at IIST Trivandrum, India. [Figure source: Class room lecture slides of AV 484 2012.]

2.3 An Example of Using MT2 Method on a Senior UG Elective Course

Here, a few examples from my past instances of successful use of MT2 method are discussed. Figure 2.2 shows the image of the slide I presented to introduce the activities that I conducted in 2012 for one of my Senior Undergraduate elective courses on Wireless Mesh Networks (AV 484) at the Indian Institute of Space science and Technology (IIST), Trivandrum. The activities comprised of three categories or tracks: (i) Lectures, (ii) Seminar, and (iii) WMN Testbed. While the name "Track" was not used in that year, that was the earliest instance of organizing a course in parallel activities which came to take a formal shape as MT2 method. In the above mentioned course, the Track-1 was the Lectures track where students are expected to attend the regular classroom lectures as prescribed by the course requirements of IIST. The syllabus for Track-1 is as provided in the **Appendix** at the end of this book. Figure 2.2 does not show the modules of the Track-1 syllabus because the figure depicts the class slides used for the first lecture during that course. Since IIST follows a practice of requiring every student to maintain a minimum attendance of 80%, I also made that as a mandatory formal requirement for the Track-1. The examinations and mark weightages required to be taken in Track-1 were also as defined by IIST guidelines. IIST prescribes two quizzes/midterm examinations (Quiz-1 and Quiz-2), to be conducted before the finals known as the end-semester examination for a semester-long course. These mid-term and finals examination requirements were also defined to be met by the main track.

In Track-2, defined as a Seminar track, I made sure every student gets a set of 3-4 research papers chosen from the digital libraries of Institution of Electrical and Electronics Engineers (IEEE) [16], Association of Computing Machinery (ACM) [1], Elsevier [12], Springer [30], or other similar high quality research publication repositories. Initial sets of papers were selected and distributed to the students. However, if the students were showing interest in papers other than what I have given them, they were gladly allowed to retain their choice. The students were monitored for the progress they made during the course work till the final evaluation of this track which was done through a class presentation where all the students and myself listened to each student for his/her presentation.

The last and final track, Track 3, was called *WMN Testbed Track* and it focused on building a real-world WMN testbed that can operate within a multi-storey academic building. Activities in this track were conducted and monitored by closely working with the students. During that year, teaching assistants were not available and as an instructor, I had carried out most of the students' training activities such as building a WMN router from scratch, making a WMN link work between two routers, forming a network by using multiple such routers, and finally, the deployment of the WMN testbed in the Aerospace (D4) building of IIST. Students did 1-2 post deployment experiments with the testbed developed as part of the WMN track testbed. At the end of the semester, I realized that the approach I used with multiple tracks was liked by the students.

2.4 Another Example Use of MT2

After using MT2 method with three tracks for the years 2012 and 2013, I tried MT2 method with four tracks in 2014 for AV 484 Wireless Mesh Networks, as depicted in Figure 2.3. The plan to introduce four tracks is due to the need I felt that students must increase their research skills. I not only encourage undergraduate research but also create venues for students to explore research in the courses I taught. While the senior UG students may not always produce visible research results such as publications, novel prototypes, or patents without significant training, occasionally, I found many of them reached very close to writing draft papers qualified for publication. In comparison, a significant number of those who took MT2-based courses published moderate quality research publications by the end of their course. More importantly, I could see many students who took MT2-based courses gained substantial experience in dissertation work, journaling their work, and methodical documentation of their work. Therefore, I found that discussing research ideas in undergraduate classes as well as introducing research-oriented tracks in MT2-based courses have a strong value in creating future scientists.

General Overview of the course: IIST AV 484 Wireless Mesh Networks (2014)

Track-1: Lectures	Track-2: Paper Writeup	Track-3: WMN Testbed	Track-4: Research Project
Attend the lectures (80% attendance required)	Review 3-4 research papers from IEEE/ACM/Elsevier digital libraries	Form teams and learn how to develop a WMN router	Develop a theory, conduct a simulation study, create a new protocol, or do something novel.
Write Quizzes (Two)	Prepare a survey writeup based on the papers	Learn how to install routing and other protocols in your router	Gather results from your study.
Write Final Exams (One)	Revise it sufficiently well to improve the quality(No plagiarism)	Learn how to build a network testbed	Evaluate the value of your results
Get sufficient points	Submit the survey report before the end of the course.	Deploy the network testbed in IIST campus.	Translate your results to publications or patents! (Optional)

Figure 2.3: Second Example of Multi-track Modular Teaching for AV 484 Wireless Mesh Networks in 2014 at IIST Trivandrum, India. [Figure source: Class rooms lecture slides of AV 484 2014.]

Due to the points mentioned above, I tried the four track program in 2014 as follows: (i) Track-1, as usual, was a Lecture track which was similar to the previous example, (ii) Track-2 focused on creating a technical writeup from selected research publications from top quality digital libraries, (iii) Track-3 focused on developing and deploying part of a research testbed called IISTMeshNet, a campus-wide WMN testbed, and (iv) Track-4 focused on research activities such as developing a new theory, conducting a simulation study with new simulation scenario, designing a new protocol, or do any similar novel work. The newly added Track-4 trained them in research activities such as creating theoretical modelling, simulation study, new protocol, or developing a novel prototype. The output of the course reflected very strongly in the final dissertation work done by the students where several students published research papers.

General overview of the course

Track-1: Lectures	Track-2: Research Paper Writeup	Track-3: Build MICRONet	Track-4: Make Docs for your Track-3 work
Attend the lectures (80% attendance required)	Review 3-4 research papers from IEEE/ACM/Elsevier digital libraries	Form teams and learn how to develop a FisherMesh router	Original Documentation for your FisherMesh router Configuration
Write Quizzes (Two)	Prepare a survey writeup based on the papers	Learn how to build a network testbed (Part of Quiz-1)	Gather results from your testbed and find observations
Write Final Exams (One)	Revise it sufficiently well to improve the quality of writeup (No plagiarism)	Implement MICRONet Testbed (Part of Quiz-2)	Document the details of the observations from the MICRONet design
Get sufficient points	Submit the survey report before the end of the course.	Deploy and test scaled version of MICRONet in IIST campus. (Final Exam)	Submit the final documentation for your part of the report.

IIST AV 484 Wireless Mesh Networks July-November 2016

Figure 2.4: Multi-track Modular Teaching Example for AV 484 Wireless Mesh Networks during 2016 at IIST Trivandrum, India. [Figure source: Class room lecture slides of AV 484 2016.]

2.5 Yet Another Example of Using MT2 Method

Based on the success of applying MT2 method over the years, I tried a few changes in 2016 in the contents of the tracks of AV 484 Wireless Mesh Networks. Figure 2.4 shows the tracks and major modules I used in 2016. The main change that I tried then was to see if the class can be trained to develop a novel network architectural system as part of an academic course work. The tracks, therefore, used in 2016 were as follows: (i) Track-1 as usual was the Lecture track which was similar to the previous examples, (ii) Track-2 focused on creating a writeup from selected research papers from top quality digital libraries in a similar way as the previous years, (iii) Track-3 focused on developing a novel software-defined network prototype system for a research and development project called MICRONet, and finally (iv) Track-4 focused on creating documentation for the work carried out as part of Track-3. Track-3 was the major focus with its objective to develop a new software-defined network prototype for a research project titled Mobile Infrastructure for Coastal Region Offshore Communications and Networks (MICRONet) funded by the Information Technology Research Academy (ITRA) [20] of Department of Science and Technology (DST), Government of India. I served as a co-investigator for the multi-university-driven MICRONet project. As part of Track-3 of the AV 484 Wireless Mesh Networks course, I had assigned the students to carry out the design of a hierarchical software-defined network architecture and prototype it. Students came out with a very interesting network prototype as the outcome of that track. One important thing to note here is that the allocation of students to the project's various roles are made by the instructor. That is, the entire class is grouped into teams and each team is assigned a specific segment in the entire development. Each team, consisting of two students, is given a specific type of node to design and implement and they are monitored for progress at regular intervals. My course teaching assistants during the course were my PhD students Sarath Babu and Abhishek Chakraborty. They both helped immensely in the follow up of those tracks. Students collectively made great progress in arriving at the prototype system by the end of the course. Therefore, it is possible to carry out novel research projects as part of a course that is based on MT2 method by carefully defining the development activity among the tracks.

2.6 Main Benefits of MT2 Method

MT2 method has many benefits. A few important benefits are listed here:

- To facilitate better and deeper learning through multiple dimensions of learning.
- Each track develops a certain direction of learning.
- Depth Vs breadth can be traded by carefully defining tracks.
- The method provides students exposure to the different aspects of learning a subject.
- The method provides a complete and richer exposure to the course topics.

- MT2 imparts all-round learning in any academic courses where deeper learning is essential.
- MT2 method benefits the most on research-oriented courses, graduate courses, senior UG courses, elective courses, or specialized programs.
- Breadth-oriented courses can use the tracks to increase the breadth when using MT2 method.

2.7 Key Challenges of MT2 Method

Despite the benefits, MT2 method also offers a certain set of challenges as follows: (i) increase in teaching workload, (ii) challenge in handling large classes, (iii) unsuitability for courses that do not need deeper learning, and (iv) mandatory teachers' expertise. Each of these issues is detailed here.

Increase in Teaching Workload

Complete involvement of a teacher is very much essential for an effective class. MT2 method helps the teachers as well as students to be completely involved or immersed in the topic through the various modalities of the tracks defined as part of the course. Therefore, MT2 method offers slightly additional workload compared to traditional (non-MT2) methodologies. However, the additional effort put in by the teachers is highly rewarded in terms of the learning outcomes of the students.

For a full time faculty in a research university, the workload can be utmost two courses for 100% effort when they teach the courses for the first time. That is, for first time courses, at least 50% effort (4 hours per work day per course) needs to be reserved. For a second time or repeat teaching of a course, only 30-33% of the time is required. Therefore, a faculty member may take utmost three courses in a given semester under MT2 method.

For a full time faculty with research and teaching responsibilities, he/she may need to reserve explicit effort for conducting research. For example, if a research and teaching faculty is allowed to spend 40% time (16 hours a week) for his/her research, then he may be allowed to take only one new course when using MT2 method. If he/she teaches repeat courses, then two courses may utmost be allowed (34% for research, and 66% for two repeat MT2 courses). Table 2.1 provides a few example situations where the workload under MT2-based courses is allowed for various example cases.

Note here that a course in this case is considered approximately 3-credits worth with at least three hours of class room instruction in a week. Such a 3-credit course requires about 40-45 lectures of 50-60 minutes each.

Table 2.1: Examples of estimated teaching workload share for MT2 method

Sl. No	Research Time	New Courses	Repeat Courses	Free time for other work
1	50% (20 hours/week)	1 (50% or 20 hours/week)	0	0%
2	40% (16 hours/week)	1 (50% or 20 hours/week)	0	10%
3	40% (16 hours/week)	0	1 (33% or 13 hours/ week)	27%
4	30% (12 hours/week)	0	2 (66%, 26 hours/week)	4%
5	0%	2 (100%, 40 hours/week)	0	0%
6	0%	0	3 (100%, 40 hours/week)	0%
7	50% (20 hours/week)	0	1 (33%, 13 hours/week)	17%

It may be possible to allow a contract teaching faculty to take three new courses under MT2 method which, however, may be requiring additional effort as well as over-time payments as stipulated by the labor laws of the land. I, however, do not advise to overload the faculty with teaching responsibilities. Overloading faculty members may have a direct impact in terms of lowering the teaching quality, thereby, invalidating the very purpose of employing them.

Challenge in Handling Very Large Classes

Another challenge of MT2 method is it needs slightly more effort than traditional teaching. Therefore, large classes are particularly loading for a faculty member to handle alone. The main workload is in the process of evaluating the performance of various tracks as well as modules within those tracks. One potential solution for solving this issue is by allotting sufficient number of Teaching Assistants (TAs) to support the faculty member in large classes. The teaching assistants shall also be familiar with the general area of the course in order to be effective. Some additional familiarization may be needed for TAs in some special courses or highly narrow elective courses. The instructor shall take the responsibility of holding training sessions for the TAs in order to manage the tracks as well as the modules within them. Table 2.2 provides an estimate of the number of teaching assistants needed for large classes under MT2 method. As presented in the table, for large classes, TA assistance is essential for conducting MT2 method effectively. Usually, senior students, particularly Masters or PhD, who are familiar with the course topics can be recruited as TAs. For every 15 students in the class, one TA is sufficient to handle the class strength. In the event of junior, temporary, guest, or contract teachers recruited to serve as TAs, then one contract/junior teacher TA per every 20 students is sufficient.

Table 2.2: Student TA allocation needed for MT2 method

Sl. No	Class Size	Number of Student TAs needed	Weekly effort needed from TAs (hours)
1	20	0	0
2	35	1	8 hours/week
3	50	2	16 hours/week
4	65	3	24 hours/week
5	>65	3+1 TA for every 15 students beyond 65	8 hours/week/TA

Unsuitability for Courses That Do Not Need Deeper Learning

There exist certain types of academic courses where MT2 method is neither suitable nor most appropriate. The courses that need a broad coverage of topics, without much depth in any one of the topics, are examples of courses where MT2 method is unsuitable. For example, consider an introductory freshman course titled *Basic Electrical Engineering* or *Basic Electronics Engineering* which are common in most undergraduate engineering curriculum. Such courses are basic and introductory courses where students need to understand the introduction to Electrical or Electronics engineering. In such introductory courses, depth is not the major objective. Therefore, MT2 method is unnecessary. Another example is *Introduction to Management Sciences* as a broad introductory course in management where deeper learning may not be intended by the curriculum designers. Wherever there is no intention to impart deeper and all-round knowledge about a subject, MT2 method is not essential.

Mandatory Teachers' Expertise

Teachers shall be well versed in the subject to effectively use MT2 method. Teachers who are constrained to do well-prepared classes, may not find it as effective as other teachers in using MT2 method. Teachers who are habituated to a very limited preparation, by way of a quick reading before their classes, cannot effectively do justice to MT2 method. Many private self-financing colleges and institutions, especially in developing countries, are constrained to hire teachers with sufficient exposure to the subjects. Such teachers, who lack expertise and are forced to teach a subject without holding good grasp, cannot effectively practice MT2 method. I had seen many such examples in developing countries where instructors are asked to teach subjects without expertise due to the shortage of teachers. However, a sincere teacher who passionately practices MT2 method can accomplish substantial expertise in teaching that subject!

2.8 Summary

In this chapter, the main concept of MT2 method is presented. One simple example as well as multiple real-world examples have been detailed in order to understand and practice the method in a university environment. A course that follows MT2 method can define a small number of activity tracks that can complement the main lecture track. The activity tracks can provide diversified and complementary information about the topics covered in the main track. MT2 method can substantially help the teaching-learning process in class-room based teaching in universities. The main benefits and the key challenges of using MT2 method were also presented.

Right education should help the student, not only to develop his capacities, but to understand his own highest interest.

- Jiddu Krishnamurti, World Renowned Philosopher.

Chapter 3
The Tracks

Beginning is easy. Continuing is hard. - Japanese Proverb.

It is important to decide on the number of tracks that is appropriate for a course under MT2 method because the number of tracks determines the effectiveness of the course. Each track demands certain type of effort from the instructor as well as the Teaching Assistants (TAs). When to create a new track? What should be the considerations for defining a track? What is the right number of tracks in a course? How should the tracks interrelate within a course? All these questions are answered and the general guidelines to be followed under the Multi-Track Modular Teaching (MT2) method for defining and maintaining tracks are presented in this chapter.

3.1 Introduction

The use of multiple tracks forms the back-bone of MT2 method. While having only one track translates the teaching to the traditional approach, an excessive number of tracks will make the course handling a very burdensome activity. Use of fewer than the right number of tracks leaves an academic course not satisfactorily benefitting from MT2 method. The use of right number of tracks can make the multi-track modular teaching method a very enriching and deeper learning approach.

Further to the number of tracks, the types of tracks forms another important factor. It is of utmost importance to define the nature of tracks based on the nature of the course offered. How to determine the effective number of tracks and character of the tracks defined are the focal topics of this chapter. A set of thumb rules, that I used, are discussed for determining the number and types of tracks that a particular academic course can use, when using MT2 method, for effective teaching-learning process.

3.1.1 Benefits of Defining Tracks

One of the questions asked by instructors and students alike when they hear about MT2 method is what are the benefits of defining tracks? The key benefit of defining tracks is that each track helps in specifically focusing on an activity that complements the lecture track. Such a focus will be greatly helpful to impart deeper and all-round knowledge about the subject. For example, assume that a course defines the following two tracks: (i) Lecture track and (ii) Writing track.

The definition of the writing track as a separate track from the lecture track clearly communicates the importance of writing as an activity with the students. On the other hand, writing as an activity can also be introduced within the course as a mixed set of assignments, however, in such a case, students may lose clarity of a framework of major focal areas. Such a lack of framework reduces the learning effectiveness. In MT2 method, the definition of tracks provides multi-modal learning approach with clarity about the structure as well as major directions of the course. The enhanced learning comes from the multi-modality of learning provided by the well-defined tracks. In fact, major activity directions that can be used in a complementary manner are suitable for defining as support tracks. I found MT2 method as a very effective tool for multi-modal teaching-learning process.

Further, in the two-track example course mentioned above, the students can focus better on the course due to the two different activity sequences within the course. Such a track definition helps better the mental preparation of students, thus leading to better outcome of the course as well as learning compared to a single track with activities combined in an inseparable manner. It is also possible to include practical or experimental tracks where some of the non-class room activity related to the courses can be introduced within a specific track of the overall course.

3.1.2 Examples of Potential Tracks in EE-CS Area

A list of example tracks that can be used for typical Electrical Engineering and Computer Science (EE-CS) curricula is provided in alphabetical order here:

- Amazon web services experiments track.
- Android mobile applications development track.
- Apple mobile application development track.
- Artificial intelligence system modeling track.
- Back-end system design track.
- C/C++ programming track.
- Chip design track.
- Cloud computing system development track.
- Cluster computing experiments track.
- Cognitive networking track.
- Compiler design track.
- Data analytics track.
- Database design and development track.
- Database implementation and performance analysis track.
- Database optimization track.
- Data structure implementation track.
- Deep learning track.
- Delay tolerant network programming track.
- Drone networks experiments track.
- Drone networks modeling and simulation track.
- E-commerce back-end design track.

- E-commerce front-end design track.
- E-commerce full stack design track.
- Firebase development experiments track.
- Full stack software development track.
- Graphical user interface development track.
- Hadoop programming track.
- High performance computing track.
- Image processing track.
- Internet-of-Things data analysis and programming track.
- Internet-of-Things system development track.
- Interplanetary networking track.
- Jupyter-based programming track.
- Long-term evolution network simulation track.
- MATLAB-based programming track.
- Machine learning track.
- Mobile ad hoc network mobility analysis track.
- Mobile ad hoc network simulation experiments track.
- Mobile ad hoc network testbed-based experiments track.
- Mobile cloud computing track.
- Mobile computing software development track.
- Network forensics track.
- Network protocol stack experiments track.
- Network security experiments track.
- Network security solution development track.

- Network simulation track in a computer networks course.
- Network testbed building track.
- Numerical C/C++ programming track.
- Numerical Python programming track.
- Optical network simulation track.
- Parallel programming track.
- Perl/Ruby programming track.
- Programming languages track.
- Python programming track.
- Real-world data collection and network modeling track in a computer networks course.
- Research literature review track.
- Robotic system prototyping track.
- SPARQL experiments track.
- Social network experiments track.
- Software defined networking track.
- Software defined wireless networking track.
- Software development track.
- Networked System prototype development track.
- TCP/UDP server implementation and optimization track.
- Text data analytics track.
- Time complexity analysis track.
- Traffic collection and analysis track in a computer networks course.
- Visual data analytics track.

- Web design track.
- Wireless body area network experiments track.
- Wireless mesh network simulation track.
- Wireless mesh network testbed development track.
- Wireless sensor network experiments track.

3.1.3 Examples of Potential Tracks in Space science and Technology Area

- Attitude and orbit control track.
- Bio-astronautics track.
- Bio-inspired structural design track.
- Communication systems design track.
- Control and guidance design track.
- Cube satellite development track.
- Delay tolerant networking track.
- Drosophila experimentation track.
- High throughput satellite design track.
- Humanoid robotics design track.
- Inter-satellite networking track.
- Interplanetary Internet track.
- Link budget analysis track.
- Nano-satellite design and development track.
- Navigation system design track.
- On-board computer design and development track.
- On-board control system design and development track.

- Propulsion system development track.
- Rover development track.
- Satellite-based Internet-of-Things track.
- Satellite bus development track.
- Satellite communications track.
- Simulation track for satellite networks.
- Space biology experiments track.
- Spacecraft bus design track.
- Spacecraft communication network track.
- Spacecraft development track.
- Spacecraft structures design track.
- Space mission design track.
- Space robotics systems track.
- Subsystems design track.
- Systems tool kit (STK) -based satellite orbit study track.

3.1.4 Examples of Potential Tracks in Management Sciences

- Blockchain-based supply chain system development.
- Complex network experiments in management studies track.
- Complex network studies on management track.
- Data analysis experiments in management.
- Data collection and analysis in management.
- Experiments on psychology in management track.
- Internet and e-commerce studies track.
- Macro-economics studies track.

- Micro-economics studies track.
- Micro-finance management track.
- Multi-level marketing studies track.
- Social network experiments in management systems track.
- Supply chain management simulation track.
- Survey experiments and data collection track.

3.1.5 Examples of Potential Tracks in Liberal Arts and Sciences Area

- Academic writing track.
- Artificial intelligence based experiments track.
- Conversational language track.
- Creative writing track.
- Field trip track for social studies.
- Foreign language track.
- Free-space optics experiments track.
- Historical data analysis track.
- Holography development track.
- Information technology-driven analysis of evolution of language track.
- Internet-based language translation track.
- Language experiments track.
- Non-fiction writing track.
- Optical experiments track.
- Quantum computing simulation track.

- Science fiction writing track.
- Scientific experiments track.
- Technical report and manual writing track.

3.1.6 Examples of Potential Tracks in Other Areas

- Applied mathematics track.
- Communications in humanities track.
- Cultural studies track.
- Literature survey for PhD students track.
- Observations in administrative efficiency track.
- Real-world mathematics data collection track.
- Resource management studies for villages track.
- Village diversity studies track.
- Village visit track.
- Visual communications track.

3.1.7 Other Possibilities for Tracks

Further to the above list of possible tracks, even research, design, engineering, or science project tracks can be defined to execute specific research projects that may be carried out as part of any funded research project, similar to the Capstone projects defined in some of the top university academic courses. For example, in AV 484 Wireless Mesh Networks conducted in 2016, one of the tracks I defined was to develop a Software-Defined Wireless Mesh Network prototype system that uses a novel hierarchical network architecture for the MICRONet project. As part of the track, students were grouped and each of the groups is assigned a part of the overall project. Students not only got exposed to the development of novel network prototypes, but also understood the process involved in the design as well as realization. As far as the effectiveness of teaching-learning process was concerned, I estimated that the use of elements of R&D projects, defined as a track, can be very useful.

3.2 Deciding the Type and Nature of Tracks

Instructor of the course is the final authority to decide on the type and nature of tracks that need to be defined as part of an MT2-based academic course. Here a brief set of guidelines is provided to help an instructor to determine the nature and type of tracks.

- All tracks shall follow the university's academic guidelines.
- In theory courses, the main track can be a lecture track for which the largest credit share can be assigned.
- All support tracks, other than the main track, shall complement the Lecture-track of the academic course.
- The tracks of an academic course shall have as minimal overlap as possible among themselves.
- The tracks of a course shall be defined in an unambiguous manner.
- The tracks shall be defined based on the instructor's plan as well as the objectives of the course.

In the following sections, each of these points is elaborated.

3.2.1 Define Tracks that Follow the University's Academic Guidelines

Every university/institute has its own policies and guidelines on curriculum, format of courses, evaluation method, and grading policies. It is important to make sure the creation of tracks does not violate the university's or institute's policy. For example, if a particular university does not allow marks to be given for non-lecture tracks, then the purpose of MT2 method will not be met. Even if a university demands strict guidelines on the mark components to be given for midterm and final examinations with no possibility for any other activities, then MT2 method cannot be attempted. It should be noted that MT2 method can be used in a university/institute that allows flexible, modern, and effective curriculum. In particular, MT2 method is most appropriate in universities that use Outcome Based Education (OBE). OBE is an educational theory where the outcomes (goals) expected from the education program defines every part of the education. That is, the outcomes expected to be accomplished in terms of the knowledge of students are used to define the methods for teaching as well as evaluation. When using MT2 for OBE, tracks can be defined based on the expected outcomes. In universities, where flexible evaluation is not allowed, the instructor shall first write to the concerned authorities in order to obtain necessary flexibility in the evaluation before using MT2 method.

3.2.2 Define Tracks to Complement the Lecture-track

The types of tracks defined by an instructor shall be based on the suitability of the tracks to complement the main lecture track. If the tracks do not complement, then the relevance and usefulness of them will be limited. Further, non-complementary tracks or highly overlapping tracks may create ambiguity. An instructor should carefully think about what tracks can complement the main track in order for deciding the track types. His/her decision can be based on the objectives of the course. For example, an academic course that is intended to provide significant practical skills shall consider introducing experimental tracks. On the other hand, an academic program that considers research publications as a complementary activity, essential for the students, may introduce an academic/technical writing, literature survey, theoretical modeling, or simulation tracks, to help impart the additional research skills. In a course where collecting data is a critically needed skill, a track that deals with research survey can be considered. In fact, many of today's courses in Computer Science and Engineering expects system development or programming skills. In such courses, a programming track can greatly help. In conclusion, the type of the tracks is decided based on the complementary nature of the track to the main track as well as the expected outcomes of the course.

3.2.3 Define Minimally Overlapping Tracks

In an academic course where there exist more than two tracks, it is important that the tracks do not overlap significantly. Due to the important need of complementary nature of tracks, there shall not be duplication of activities. Duplication of tracks' activities results in wasted time and resources while reducing the impact of each track. In addition, students' respect, interest, and dedication for the tracks may be affected when tracks have significant overlap.

3.2.4 Define Unambiguous Tracks

It is important to define the tracks, in an unambiguous manner, during the initial introductory phase of the course. Students who undertake an MT2-based course shall be communicated about the number as well as the types of tracks. Plans for each track shall be briefly communicated to the students in a clear manner. While it is acceptable to delay the discussion on finer details of the tracks and modules to later classes, clarity on the overall objectives of each track shall be communicated sufficiently early in the course. Further, it is also acceptable to make some changes during the execution of the course, even though a class is given sufficient explanation of various activities of each track. In conclusion, definition of tracks shall be clear and unambiguous.

3.2.5 Define Tracks Based on the Instructor's Plan for the Course

Instructor's plan for an academic course is prime in the definition of the tracks. The number and types of tracks shall be announced early in the course. In universities that follow Outcome-Based Evaluation (OBE) schemes, the tracks may be defined according to the learning outcome expected from the course. For example, the course expects to gather a lot of practical skills, then outcome based evaluation shall include examinations/questions/viva-voce evaluations/projects/presentations based on the evaluation of expected practical skills among the students. In many countries, academic agencies that govern the education system follow outcome-based evaluation. For example, in India the All India Council for

Technical Education (AICTE) [3] recently suggested outcome based evaluation in technical institutions across India. Once the instructor's plan for the course is determined, he/she should creatively design the types of tracks needed to accomplish his/her teaching plan. Instructor shall ensure that the tracks are conducted satisfactorily well during the course.

3.3 How Many Tracks?

One of the important questions that an instructor faces, when he/she decides to use MT2 method, is the number of tracks he/she should use. While there exist no hard rules on the number of tracks that can be used in an academic course, certain thumb rules and general guidelines can help define the number of tracks in a course under MT2 method. Before proceeding with the discussion on the thumb rules, the following important points are to be noted before deciding on the number and types of tracks: (i) Essentiality of a track, (ii) Minimality of tracks, (iii) Clarity of tracks, and (iv) Complementarity of tracks. Each of these points is elaborated here.

3.3.1 Essentiality of a Track

A new track shall be defined, in addition to the main lecture track, only if it is truly essential and there exists a requirement for the track to continue for at least more than half the duration of the academic course. In simpler terms, only for a complementary academic activity that spans for the entire duration or at least more than half the duration of the course, a new track can be defined. A minor programming exercise that an instructor wants his/her students to develop as a onetime activity or submission may not be a good choice to be defined as a track unless the activity spans through the major portion of the course. Further, the activity shall be substantial in content in order to be considered for a track. In conclusion, a track shall be defined only when it is necessary, essential, and spans for a major duration of the course.

3.3.2 Minimality of Tracks

While the exact number of tracks within a course under MT2 method is determined by the instructor, the number of tracks shall be as minimal as possible. A large number of tracks can be adding more overhead than the value achieved. Similarly, a lower than necessary number of tracks will not provide the benefits of MT2 method. By following the empirical rules of thumb or guidelines, an instructor will be able to decide on the number of tracks he/she needs to use for effective teaching learning process.

In one of my course on Wireless Mesh Networks conducted in 2012, I used three tracks that worked very effectively. I modified the tracks subsequent years in order to make four tracks. I found that four tracks were also useful and effective. However, adding, more than four tracks in a semester or quarter long course is to be considered carefully, even though a maximum of six tracks can be accommodated. I most often use three or four tracks in my courses.

In a 1-credit semester-long course, with approximately 15 hours where each lecture hour is 50-60 minutes, I recommend to have utmost two tracks only. For a 2-credit semester-long course, with 30 lectures, utmost three tracks can be considered. Similarly, in a 3-credit course, an instructor can use 3-4 tracks easily. For 4-credit courses of length spanning a semester, we may consider more than four tracks. My own experience provided me with good confidence on the empirically optimal number of 3-4 tracks for any 3-4 credit courses. Compared to all the semester or quarter-long courses, some universities run year-long courses or training programs. Such year-long programs can have up to a maximum of one dozen carefully designed tracks if the instructor desires to do so.

3.3.3 Clarity of a Track's Objectives

Clarity of a track is another important aspect of a track. Clarity of a track refers to that the objectives of the track shall be clear and well-defined. First, the instructor should have a clear understanding and plan about each of the tracks. Further, he should communicate the objectives of each track effectively to the students. In the first lecture of the course, indications about the number of tracks and their objectives may be discussed with the students. While the complete details of the tracks are not required to be communicated to the students in the first class, one of the subsequent lectures can be used to communicate the plans for each track to them in an unambiguous manner. Students, most often, come with doubts and questions on the concept of the tracks as well as the reason for the choice of tracks. The instructor shall be prepared to provide clear examples of benefits that each of the tracks may add to their studies. For example, in 2-3 courses where I had introduced the activity of writing as a separate track, students had difficulty in understanding the value of such a track in an academic course. My explanations, with several examples, of how writing track adds value to them in the subject they study, not only clear their doubts but also elevate them to a separate level of perception. If an instructor is not satisfactorily answering the reasons behind introduction of a particular track, students may not appreciate his/her intention sufficiently well.

While communicating the track's objectives, the details of the modules within a track need not be revealed completely to the students at the beginning of the course. That is, certain amount of surprise elements may be maintained within the modules. Therefore, the objectives of the track shall be clearly defined and communicated to the students while maintaining the surprise elements of certain modules within the track.

Consider one example from the course AV 484 Wireless Mesh Networks that I had conducted during July-November 2018 semester at IIST. The student teams were organized to develop a wireless mesh network testbed in the following sequence: (i) router building, (ii) link formation, (iii) network formation, and (iv) network experiments to be conducted over the full scale network. The finer details of the tasks were revealed only just before the conduct of activities of those modules. The final module and associated activities were also not detailed sufficiently well in order to maintain the surprise, until prior to those activities. We conducted 1-2 special discussion sessions to explain the final activity session. Students felt very surprised when they actually carried out the last full scale experiments session. Figure 3.1 shows the illustration distributed to the students describing the sequence of the last activity module and the actions to be carried out as part of the Track-3 (to build a segment of IISTMeshNet) of the course I conducted during that semester.

AV484: Wireless Mesh Networks
Track - 3
Experiment Plan for Performance Analysis of Wireless Mesh Network Testbed in D3 Building

	Time -->						
0 - 1 hr	**Continuous Activity**						
Setting up routers and laptops	**Team - 1:** Traffic monitoring and analysis. Use ***tcpdump*** for traffic collection.						
	Team - 2: Network topology data collection and analysis. Use ***wget*** utility with OLSR to collect the topology.						
	Team - 3: Analysis of packet traffic, data rate, RSSI, and link availability. Use ***tcpdump***for traffic collection. You can use the data collected by other teams for analysis.						
	Team - 4: Overall coordination of the Track-3 activity.						
	Team - 10: Analysis of link cost using link metric provided by OLSR protocol. Use ***wget*** utility with OLSR to link cost information.						
	Team - 5	**Team - 6**	**Team - 7**	**Team - 8**	**Team - 9**	**Group Mobility**	**Random Mobility**
	TCP throughput measurement using ***iperf*** utility (5 sessions per node pair) 1. Between 1-hop nodes 2. Between farthest nodes 3. Decide other node pairs	UDP throughput measurement using ***iperf*** utility (5 sessions per node pair) 1. Between 1-hop nodes 2. Between farthest nodes 3. Decide other node pairs	Delay measurement using ***ping*** utility 1. Between 1-hop nodes 2. Between farthest nodes 3. Decide other node pairs	VoIP throughput measurement using ***D-ITG*** utility 1. Between 1-hop nodes 2. Between farthest nodes 3. Decide other node pairs	FTP characteristics analysis using ***SimpleHTTPServer*** and ***lftp*** utility	One laptop from each team should participate in group mobility experiment. + TCP througput analysis between two node pairs by Team - 5 + UDP througput analysis between two node pairs by Team - 6	One laptop from each team should participate in random mobility experiment. + TCP througput analysis between two node pairs by Team - 5 + UDP througput analysis between two node pairs by Team - 6

Figure 3.1: Illustration of activities carried out as part of one of the final modules of Track-3 (Build a Segment of IISTMeshNet) of AV 484 Wireless Mesh Networks course in 2018.

There were a total of about 10 teams, each of 3-5 students, as shown in Figure 3.1. Each team has been given a responsibility during the deployment as part of the final experiments activity. Teams 1-4 and 10 had been given the activity that spans throughout the period of experiment. Teams 5-9 carried out experiments in sequence as shown in the Figure 3.1. During our discussions about the activity, we did not give much thrust to the excitement involved in the activity in order to allow them to experience the fun in the activity. Students not only successfully built a wireless mesh network of about 30 router nodes in our academic building, but also conducted a variety of experiments over it. The last two experiments, during which the mobility experiments were carried out, were somewhat surprising to the students when they were actually carried out. Only prior to the deployment and experiment module of the Track-3, we revealed the details of the activities to a detailed extend. Thus, the mobility experiments were a big surprise for them when they actually carried out. Such elements of surprise motivate the students beyond our expectation and make the students very much interested in the course.

In conclusion, the instructor shall have good clarity about activities planned for a track in order to ensure success of a track. Ambiguity of the tracks will create confusion among the students, thereby, leading to ineffective use of MT2 method. Elements of surprise about a particular step within an activity module can be made, thereby, enhancing students' interest.

3.3.4 Complementarity of Tracks

A track shall minimize the overlap with the rest of the tracks. That is, every track in a course, following MT2 approach, shall be complementary to each other. One of the main objectives of MT2 is to ensure deep and all-round learning on a particular academic course. By ensuring a set of complementary tracks, we can make sure to benefit from the various directions of learning about the subject. Complementarity[1] of a track is required to ensure multiple dimensions of learning. For example, the objectives or the modules defined in the support tracks shall complement the theoretical lessons learned in the main Lecture track. Consider a two track course where a Lecture track and Experiments track are used. The

Experiments track activities may be chosen in such a way that some of the topics covered in the Lecture track could be considered for experimental validation in the experimental track. Therefore, the activities in the Experiments track enhance and complement the theoretical knowledge gained from the main Lecture track.

A non-track based system where many activities are mixed together may result in ambiguity and lack of clarity, thereby, resulting in limited or incomplete learning.

3.4 When to Define New Tracks?

When the instructor feels that specific direction of learning is important for better teaching-learning process in a course the instructor handles, he could utilize MT2 approach by creating necessary tracks. For example, consider a course where there exists only one track, addition of a second track can be conducted if the instructor expects the students to gain from a very important and clearly defined related activity. That is, consider a Biology course with two existing tracks: Lecture track and Experiments track. If the instructor genuinely feels that students should develop excellent skills for observations, then he can create a new third track titled Observations. The Observations track can focus on observing the nature or any other biological objects and make notes as per the instructor's plan. There are several benefits that the instructor creates for the students in adding such a third, Observations, track. Some of the benefits are the following: (i) Even though observation activity is present in the Experiments track, creating a separate Observations track can highlight the need for a student to become a good observer as well as note taker and (ii) While the Experiments track focuses more on the outcomes of the experiments and less on observations, the Observations track can completely focus on the activity of observation as well as noting. Therefore, having a third Observations track can be beneficial in such a case. In conclusion, based on the specific direction of learning, as the instructor decides for a course, appropriate tracks can be created.

In universities where the outcome-based evaluation scheme is in practice, the decision to create the tracks can be determined based on the outcome expected from the course. An instructor who practices MT2 method can make a genuine decision on creating a new track based on the instructor's objectives for the skills expected by the students to develop.

3.5 Feasibility of Tracks

One important decision that an instructor must be aware in practicing MT2 method is the evaluation of feasibility of the tracks he/she creates for an academic program. A feasible and small number of tracks can be sufficient in deriving the benefits of MT2 method. I found that conducting an academic course with only one track, as in traditional non-MT2 approaches, does not benefit the pedagogical process as much as an MT2-based course benefits. On the other hand, a course with numerous tracks will be cumbersome and heavy for the instructors to conduct. Therefore, a small number of tracks, that are feasible for the instructor to conduct, is most appropriate. For 3-credit semester-long courses that I conducted over the last 8-9 years, I found no reason to go beyond four tracks. All my course requirements have been met either with three or four tracks. Therefore, I suggest 2-4 tracks are sufficient for most academic courses of 3-4 credits.

3.6 Assigning Credits for Tracks

Once the tracks are defined, instructor shall think about the credits/points per track that can be assigned. The credit distribution among the tracks shall be based on the importance of the track within a course. For example, consider an academic course where the main track holds more importance. In such a semester-long academic course with three credits, one credit can be assigned to the supporting tracks, whereby, the main lecture track will retain two credits. Similarly, in a four credit course where the credit distribution is such that three credits are assigned for the course and one credit is meant for tutorials, then, two credits out of the total can be assigned for the support tracks. Even in a two credit course, one or half credit can be assigned to the support tracks.

The credit distribution across tracks can be uniformly distributed if all the tracks are of equal importance. For most academic courses where practical training is of equal importance as that of the theoretical knowledge, then the main lecture track can be given similar credits as that of the support tracks. For example, consider a Clinical Psychology course of three credits worth where the main track is a lecture track and the support tracks include a Clinical Observation track and Clinical Practice track. In such a case, same preference as well as credits can be given for both the support tracks as well as lecture track by assigning one credit each.

While an instructor may take a final decision on the credit distribution for a course conducted using MT2 method, he shall follow all the rules and regulations of the university/institute for the credit distribution.

In the situation where credits are not easy to be divided between various tracks of an MT2-based course, points or marks can be assigned to various modules of the tracks. For example, in one of the 3-credit courses on computer networks that I conducted in IIST, there were three tracks defined as follows: (i) Lecture track, (ii) Writing track, and (iii) Innovative Project track. I have assigned 67 points/marks for the Lecture track, the main track in the course, and the rest of the points is divided at 10 and 23 points/marks between the Writing and Innovative Project tracks, respectively, which were considered as important supporting tracks. It can, therefore, be seen that the credit distribution resulted in 2.01, 0.3, and 0.69 credits, respectively, for the Lecture, Writing, and Innovative Project tracks in that course.

3.7 Types of Tracks

Based on the synchronization characteristics, tracks in MT2 method can be classified into three categories: Synchronous, Semi-synchronous, and Asynchronous tracks. In a synchronous track, all the track's modules are to be synchronized with one or more of the remaining tracks. On the other hand, in Semi-synchronous tracks, only some modules of the track have synchronization requirements with modules of other tracks. In comparison to these two types of tracks, an Asynchronous track is defined as a track with activity modules that are not synchronized with the modules in other tracks. Each of these types of tracks is briefed here and the detailed discussion on modules related to track synchronization can be found in Chapter 4.

3.7.1 Synchronous Tracks

Contents of a track consist of a set of activity modules that may have some dependency relationship with other modules in other tracks. For example, consider a 2-track course with the main track as Lecture track and the support track as Experiments track. If there is any dependency between modules of the Experiments track with the Lecture tracks, then there exist some synchronization requirements to be met for the Experiments track's activity modules. That is, Synchronous tracks are the tracks that have modules which are dependent on the modules of other tracks. For example, in the case mentioned above, the modules of the Experiments track can be started only after completing certain modules of the Lecture track.

3.7.2 Semi-synchronous Tracks

Semi-synchronous tracks have some modules dependent on the modules of other tracks and the rest of the modules independent. Compared to the above mentioned Synchronous tracks, the Semi-synchronous tracks do not have strict dependency of modules of a track with the modules of the other tracks. For example, consider the case of a 2-track MT2-based Management course where the main track is Lecture track and the supporting track is Surveying track that deals with conducting marketing surveys. Imagine that the Surveying track has six modules. The first two modules can be initiated without waiting for completion of any of the modules in the Lecture track. However, certain advanced activity modules, such as an online social network survey, in the Surveying track may have to wait till completion of some of the Lecture track modules. In such as case, we can consider the Survey track as a Semi-synchronous track due to the fact that only some modules depend on completion of certain Lecture track modules.

3.7.3 Asynchronous Tracks

Asynchronous tracks have all the modules in them independent of modules of other tracks. Therefore, asynchronous tracks have most flexibility in conducting the modules. It is also possible to easily reorder the activity modules because they are not dependent on other tracks. The best example for this type of tracks is the main track, usually a Lecture track, that does not depend on other tracks in most cases of MT2-based courses that I practiced.

3.8 Summary

One of the key aspects of MT2 method is the multiple tracks of learning that enable deep and multi-dimensional learning. It is important to define the tracks properly and effectively to ensure successful use of MT2 method. This chapter explained the key aspects required for deciding the types and number of tracks. Tracks shall: (i) follow the university/institute's academic policies and guidelines, (ii) complement each other or support the main track, Lecture-track in most cases, of the academic course, (iii) have minimal overlap among themselves, (iv) be defined based on the instructor's plan for the course, and (v) be defined in an unambiguous manner. The number of tracks can be decided based on (i) essentiality of a track, (ii) minimality of tracks, (iii) objective clarity of tracks, and (iv) complementarity of tracks. Based on the dependency of a track's content activities with the rest of the tracks, a track may be categorized as (i) Synchronous, (ii) Semi-synchronous, or (iii) Asynchronous track.

As you teach, you learn. - Jewish Proverb.

Chapter 4
The Modularity

The highest education is that which does not merely give us information but makes our life in harmony with all existence.
- Rabindranath Tagore, Indian Poet and Nobel Prize Winner.

4.1 Introduction

Once the tracks are identified, the next is modular design of the tracks in Multi-Track Modular Teaching (MT2) method. While each track deals with a specific and complementary activity, it is important to provide certain modularity within each of the tracks. Modularity refers to the modular format of activities within each of the tracks. That is, the activities in a track are organized as a set of modules, each of which can be separately completed by the students and are, therefore, separately evaluated by the instructors. The need for modularity and various aspects related to the modularity are discussed in this chapter.

The modularity implementation depends on the type of the track, topic covered in the track, feasibility of modularization, and most importantly the plan of the instructor. Note that the main track, usually a Lecture track, is defined by a curricula and syllabi in all universities, institutes, and colleges. In some universities, the course syllabus is already defined in modules in terms of chapters or units. In fact, the syllabus organization in most courses indicates modularity as one of the important aspects. Therefore, we discuss only the modularity of support tracks 2 to N in an N-track MT2-based course when the first track is typically a lecture track.

Each of the tracks 2 to N, in an N-track course, is modularly designed when using MT2 method. That is, activities as part of those tracks are defined into a set of clearly defined modules such that each module can be completed and evaluated. Further, the difficulty levels for modules can be carefully designed so that students may accomplish a modular and enhanced learning experience.

4.2 Why Modularity?

In MT2 method, modularity of a track is defined as the way contents or activities of the track is grouped into modules such that effective teaching and learning can be achieved. It is important to understand why a modular approach is required. The main reasons for utilizing a modular approach for each of the tracks are the following:

- Better understanding of the topics of the track
- Adaptability and customization of the track
- Simplifying the grading process
- Making the tracks more interesting
- Achieving better track synchronization

Each of these aspects is discussed in detail here.

4.2.1 Better Understanding of the Topics of the Track

Modularity helps improve the students' understanding of the subject taught using MT2 method. Students learn the courses better with modular grouping of the topics covered in the class. Modularity breaks down the otherwise monolithic content defined by a typical course's syllabus to various logical modules where the completion and grading process for each module can be easily accomplished. Grouping of activities can be made logically comprehensible to arrive at a single module while enabling better understanding for students. Further, such multiple modules can be organized in order to progressively improve the logical organization of modules and difficulty levels within a track. Finally, it is important to be able to evaluate the activity modules independently. Modularity helps on all the above matters.

4.2.2 Adaptability, Flexibility, and Customization of the Tracks

Organizing the contents/activities as modules within the tracks helps the students to learn better through a stage by stage manner. That is, after finishing one module in a particular track, the students can proceed to approach the next module in the track. Further, it is possible to adapt the contents of one module based on how the previous modules have been completed by the students. Thus the modularity provides high adaptability of the track's contents during the progress of the academic course. That means, based on the learning ability of students, we can adaptively add or delete modules. If the class is proven to be performing better than expected, additional challenging modules can be included. Similarly, if the class finds the topics harder or when there is shorter time left for the course completion, suitably some harder modules within the track can be excluded. An instructor may take such decisions based on the benefit that the class gets by making the course so mid-course customized.

Modularity helps, further, to have *optional modules* that can be provided only to the fast learners of a class while the rest of the class may proceed with the regular and mandatory modules. In some of the classes, exceptionally brilliant students may need to be allowed to proceed at their own pace. In fact, in most gifted and talented education systems of the world[1], the teaching system allows students to learn at their pace.

Another benefit of modularity is the customization of the track by students themselves. For example, an instructor may define several modules of which students may need to take only a limited subset. Consider a programming class where the instructor defines a Programming track as part of the course. The instructor may define various programming modules such as *Application programming, System programming, and Mobile computing programming* where a student may take a customized set of modules as per his/her choice. A student who has more interest in Application programming may choose the modules belonging to that area. On the other hand, someone who has interest towards the System programming may choose the modules in that category. Consider another example, where a Machine learning class with an Application track in which modules are defined in areas such as *Machine learning for image processing, Machine learning for video processing, Machine learning for social networks, and Machine learning for communications*. In such a case, students may choose a customized set of modules in order to focus their application area in any one of the above mentioned areas.

Modularity, in MT2 method, helps in bringing adaptability, flexibility, as well as customization within the tracks.

4.2.3 Simplifying the Grading Process

Another benefit of the modularity of the tracks is it simplifies the grading process. That is, the students or group of students may complete a module to obtain full credits for that module. However, other modules where students make partial or no progress can be separately evaluated and credited. Thus, modularity helps in better evaluation of the performance of the students within each track. Each module can be allotted certain points/credits for completing them successfully. Immediate announcement of the module accomplishments and associated credits/points will help motivate the students greatly.

4.2.4 Making the Tracks More Interesting

Modularity makes the tracks more interesting for students in comparison to a continuous stream of activities without modularity. Further, modularity helps towards growing the difficulty or complexity level of tasks. For example, the modules for an experimental track of a wireless mesh networking course, that I had conducted in 2014, had employed the following sequence: (i) creation of router nodes[2], (ii) link level experiments requiring two nodes, (iii) small scale network level experiments requiring less than half a dozen nodes, and (iv) full scale network level experiments with all available nodes. Such a sequence of modularized activities within the track gives students substantial interest and engagement in a track's activities. A teacher is successful when he/she is able to provide high interest and engagement, in students, towards the course's topics. Further, defining modules can help the students to obtain the feeling of accomplishments as the students progress through each module. Such feeling of intermediate accomplishments may greatly improve the confidence level as well as learning of the students.

4.2.5 Achieving Better Track Synchronization

Track synchronization, discussed first in Section 3.7, refers to the requirements of modules of a certain track to follow the progress of modules of another track. For example, consider an academic course where there exist two tracks: (i) Lecture track and (ii) Writing track. Some of the activities defined as part of the writing track may have to wait till certain portions in the Lecture track get completed. That is, assume that the first writing track activity can be started only after the first module of the Lecture track is completed. As discussed earlier in this chapter, synchronization refers to the situation that the activities defined as part of one track can be carried out only after completion of another module of another track.

Modularity of tracks helps in ensuring better synchronization between tracks. For example, in the above mentioned two track course, assume that the first module of the writing track can be conducted only after the completion of certain topics in the Lecture track. In a track that does not follow the modularity approach, the activities are continuous in nature and, therefore, synchronization becomes very difficult.

Consider another example of an academic course on Sociology where there are two tracks: (i) Lecture track and (ii) Survey track. The Lecture track may have a set of modules covering various aspects of sociology. The Survey track may have defined activities such as surveying various data sets belonging to the subject of Sociology. Assume that the Lecture track has five major modules and the Survey track has defined only three modules. First Survey track module is for surveying of a neighborhood society. Second is a campus-wide survey and the third is a survey about an online social network. Since the first two modules of the Survey track can be conducted early in the course work whereas the third module can be conducted only after completing the relevant, online social network-related, topics in the Lecture track. Therefore, modularizing of the track's contents can help in ensuring proper synchronization between tracks.

4.3 Choice of Modules in a Track

An instructor shall make careful choice for a track when using MT2 method. There can be a variety of modules implemented in different approaches in a given track. Here we discuss three major aspects based on which the choice of modules can be made for a track: (i) Synchrony of modules, (ii) Large Vs Small modules, and (iii) Many vs Small number of modules. Each of these issues is explained in what follows.

4.3.1 Synchrony of Modules

Synchronization is all about meeting the module dependency requirements. Not all modules in a given track may need synchronization. Modules of a track can be either synchronous, semi-synchronous, or asynchronous modules based on whether the execution of one module in a given track has any dependency on any modules in another track. That is, beginning the execution of a module within a given track may have a dependency on the completion of another module in another track. In such cases, the modules are said to be synchronous. On the other hand, in the case of asynchronous modules, each module in the given track is independent of the modules in other tracks. The decision on whether to have synchronous or asynchronous modules can be made by the instructor based on the type of course, types of modules, difficulty levels of the modules, and requirement of completion of certain syllabus portions.

Synchronous Modules

Synchronous modules within a track may have dependency of certain track modules in other tracks. Consider an example where the Track-1 deals with a Lecture track and Track-2 deals with an Experiments track. The modules in Experiments track may have certain dependency on the coverage of topics in the Lecture track. That is, the given module which has a dependency on another module, cannot begin until the completion of the other module. Therefore, certain experimental modules in Track-2 may have to synchronize with or wait for completion of the portions covered in Track-1. Instructor shall carefully consider such dependencies and order the modules in each track so that students will maximize their learning benefit. If all the modules in a track are synchronous modules, then that track can be considered as a Synchronous track as briefly discussed in Chapter 3. Note further that the definition of synchronous or asynchronous modules is based only on inter-track module dependencies. Within any given track, the modules shall be organized in strict sequence. Completion of one module within a given track is mandatory for beginning the subsequent module.

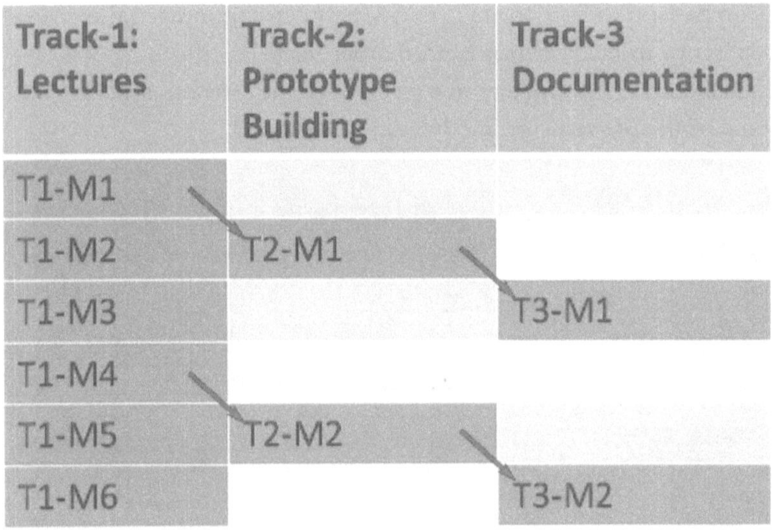

Figure 4.1: An Illustration of Synchronous Modules in MT2 Method.

Figure 4.1, shows an illustration of synchronous modules in a track where an example three-track course is shown. The Track-1 is Lecture track, Track-2 is Prototype building track, and Track-3 is Documentation track. It is important to define the Documentation track separately in order to identify and clearly communicate the importance of the documentation activity as part of the course. As per the Documentation track, an instructor may require the students to prepare technical documentation of the experimental prototypes developed as part of the Track-2, Prototype building track. As can be seen from the figure, marked with arrows, the module M-1 of Track-3 is dependent on completion of the module M-1 of Track-2. The completion of the module at the tail of the arrow is a pre-requisite to the beginning of the module at the head of the arrow. In other words, the module at the head of the arrow is dependent on the module at the tail of the arrow. Similarly, the module M-2 of Track-3 (T3-M2) requires the completion of module M-2 of Track-2 (T2-M2). The module T2-M2 is a prerequisite for the module T3-M2. If all the modules in a track have dependencies to any other tracks' modules, then the entire track is called a Synchronous track. In this case, Tracks-2 and -3 have all synchronous modules, therefore, the Tracks-2 and -3 are synchronous tracks.

Semi-synchronous Modules

In comparison to Synchronous tracks, Semi-synchronous tracks have only a subset of modules dependent on other tracks' modules. That is, only a small number of modules in a given track may have to synchronize with some of the pre-requisite modules in other tracks.

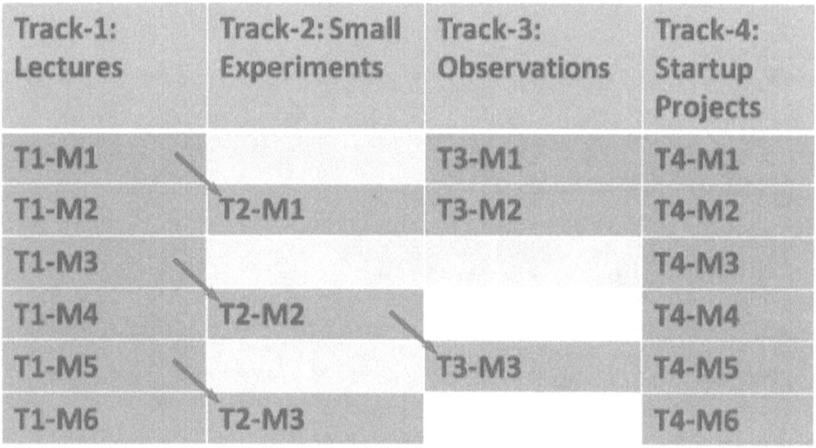

Figure 4.2: An Illustration of Semi-synchronous and Asynchronous Modules in MT2 Method.

Consider an academic course with the following four tracks as illustrated in Figure 4.2: Lectures form the Track-1, Small experiments form the Track-2, Observations are categorized as the Track-3, and finally the Track-4 deals with Startup projects. In the figure, the synchronization dependencies are marked with directed arrows. All the modules in the Small experiments track have synchronization requirements with the topics covered in the Track-1. Similarly, Track-4 has no dependency with any of the modules in other tracks. In comparison, the Track-3 has only one module (T3-M3) with dependency on one of the modules (T2-M2) in Track-2. Therefore, Track-3 is a semi-synchronous track. The instructor who handles the course can decide on the synchronization characteristics of the modules. Based on the synchronization characteristics, the modules in each track can be scheduled. In the example course depicted in Figure 4.2, modules in Track-3 can be considered as a Semi-synchronous modules.

Asynchronous Modules

Asynchronous modules are those modules in the tracks that have no dependency relationship with other modules of other tracks in an academic course that use MT2 method. Asynchronous modules are easier to schedule within the track as they need not wait for the completion of the pre-requisite modules in other tracks. However, note that within a track, modules are conducted in sequence. Therefore, the previous modules within the track shall be completed before beginning a particular module. In any case, only one module will be conducted at any time in a given track. In the example course discussed above (Figure 4.2) where there are four tracks, Tracks-1 and -4 are asynchronous.

4.3.2 Large Vs Small Modules

The size of the module in a track assumes significance in ensuring effective learning as well as handling of the track. A very large sized module can defeat the purpose of modularity. At the same time, very small sized modules can result in a track containing large number of modules, thereby, leading to difficulty in managing the modules. It is best to target moderate size for each module. Any module/task that requires less than one hour of effort is small sized module/task and the modules that require 1-4 hours can be considered as medium sized modules. The tasks that can be accomplished in 4-5 hours of effort can be considered as a moderate sized module and the tasks/modules that need more than 5 hours of effort can be considered as large modules. Exceptions on the size of a module may be considered in special cases where a larger task cannot be split into smaller units. In such cases one or two modules of large size (>5 hours of effort) can also be considered in a course as deemed fit by the instructor. The type and size of modules will be best decided based on the characteristics of the academic course for which MT2 method is employed.

4.3.3 Many Vs Small Number of Modules

Another major issue that the instructors may face during the decision on the design of a track as well as modularity of the tracks is the number of modules to be used in a track. While a single module results in completely excluding the modularity concept, a large number of modules increases the complexity of management of course, grading, and keeping track of the modules for the entire class. Therefore, it is best to consider a moderate number of modules per track. Typically, less than or equal to half a dozen modules will provide a satisfactory modularity in a track. In some of my courses, 3-4 modules proved very effective in some of the Writing tracks, whereas 4-6 modules were needed for Prototype building, Network testbed experiments, or other Hands-on experiments tracks. The number of modules in a track can be utmost 10 in a quarter or semester-based academic course. In exceptional and long-duration academic courses, such as year-long courses, the number of modules can be suitably increased to a number more than a dozen. Course instructor can make appropriate decisions on the number of modules required for such courses keeping the spirit of MT2 method in mind.

4.4 Designing Difficulty Levels of Modules

A very important factor in designing the modules and their sequencing is to determine the organization of the difficulty levels of modules. An instructor can design the difficulty levels of modules of a track in multiple ways: (i) Constant Difficulty Levels, (ii) Progressive Difficulty Levels, and (iii) Variable Difficulty Levels.

4.4.1 Modules of Constant Difficulty Levels

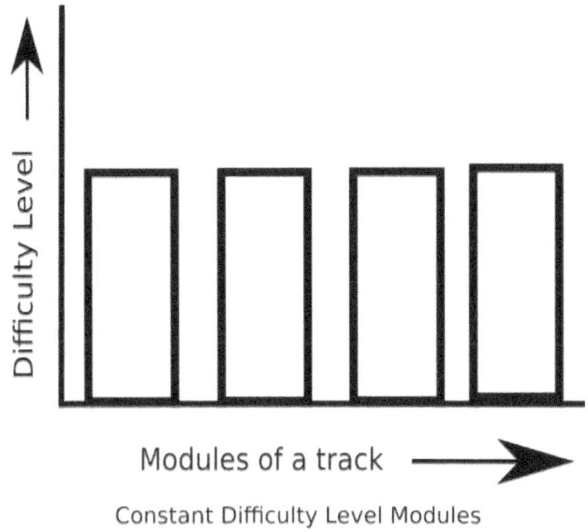

Figure 4.3: An Illustration of Difficulty Level of Modules in a Track.

In this case, the modules of a track can be of constant difficulty levels or similar difficulty levels. Figure 4.3 depicts the modules of constant difficulty level. For a given track, the difficulty levels can, sometimes, be set at almost the same difficulty level. For example, consider an academic course on Sociology that utilizes MT2 method. The instructor who handles the course may consider introducing a track on conducting sociological surveys, named Survey track. As an example, assume that he created three modules in the Survey track based on the community within the campus that the student teams should conduct the surveys: (i) faculty survey, (ii) staff survey, and (iii) student survey. Imagine that the number of samples identified for survey is similar among these three survey modules. In such a case, the difficulty levels of the three modular survey track cannot be very different. It can, therefore, be said that the modules in such a track are of constant difficulty levels.

The key benefit of designing modules with constant difficulty levels is that the modules, collectively, allow a larger task to be accomplished. For example, in the above considered course on Sociology, the Survey track was mainly meant for familiarizing the students with the process of conducting survey, analyzing the results, as well as preparing the reports. However, by modularizing the track in three modules, the larger task of a campus-wide survey is broken down into smaller difficulty levels that can be easily accomplished. Besides, during the first module of faculty survey, students get familiarized with the process of surveying, thereby, the subsequent modules can be accomplished more comfortably.

The main problem with modules of constant difficulty levels is that as the students progress through the track's modules, the later modules may appear simpler, thereby, students may feel that the modules are repetitive, less-challenging, and, in some cases, below their ability level. Instructors shall aim at avoiding such issues by avoiding repetition of modules, when considering the difficulty levels at similar levels among the modules.

4.4.2 Modules of Progressive Difficulty Levels

In this case, the difficulty level of the modules within a track are progressively increased as the track progresses as can be seen from the depiction in Figure 4.4, showing the difficulty levels of modules of a track. It is logical and useful to consider progressively increasing the difficulty levels as the students learn a track's contents. Unlike the previous case where the difficulty levels of modules are almost constant, here the modules grow in their difficulty levels such that it can maintain the challenge to the students' intellectual levels as the course progresses.

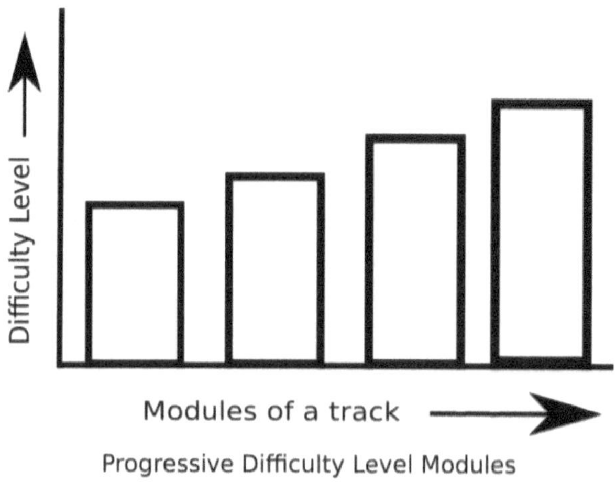

Figure 4.4: An Illustration of Difficulty Level of Modules in a Track.

Consider one of the experimental tracks that I used in my Wireless Mesh Networks course at IIST. The experimental track is meant for familiarizing the students on the development, deployment, and performance evaluation of a wireless mesh network. I have designed the track with the following modules: (i) wireless mesh router development, (ii) wireless mesh link formation between two routers, (iii) wireless mesh network formation among multiple routers, (iv) performance measurement trial experiment, and (v) full scale network deployment and performance measurement in one of our academic buildings. In the sequence of modules that I designed, there has been a progressive increase of the activity's characteristics or difficulty levels as far the network experiments are considered. Of course, the first task of developing a router was a different task module compared to the rest of the modules. Despite that task, the logical progression of the difficulty levels of the modules provides a monotonically increasing difficulty as well as complexity levels, thereby, maintaining the intellectual challenge on the students during the track's progress. I have noticed that students get excited as the modules grow in their complexity while they still can overcome.

It is essential that every module should have a progressive increase of difficulty level compared to its prior module within the track. All the modules, including the last one, in a track must have the progressive difficulty levels, only then they can be considered as the modules of progressive difficulty levels.

4.4.3 Modules of Variable Difficulty Levels

Unlike the above two categories of modules, a track can also have variable difficulty levels. That is, the modules in such a track have varying difficulty levels, however, without any particular progressive order. Some modules may be more complex than the others in terms of complexity. Due to the mix of difficulty levels of modules, no particular pattern of complexity can be observed as the course progresses.

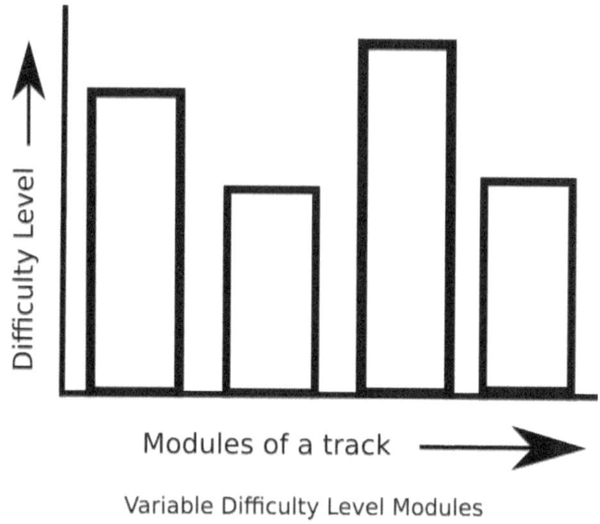

Figure 4.5: An Illustration of Difficulty Level of Modules in a Track.

Figure 4.5 shows an illustration of difficulty levels of modules of a given track. For an example, consider the track of a potential course, associated with Compilers, titled Compiler Design Track. Compiler is a computer program that translates a high level software program to a machine level code that can be executed in a digital computer. For example, the Programming languages C or C++ are high level languages that are enormously popular among computer programmers for creating both application programs as well as systems programs. A program that is written according to the syntax of C/C++ is called a high level program. Such a high level program cannot be directly executed in a computer as the computer's processor does not understand the syntax and semantics of the C/C++ language. Therefore, a program or a set of programs called compilers are designed to translate the high level program to a machine-executable program. Assume that the track for Compiler design in the course has the following six modules: (i) Module-1: Lexical Analyzer Design and development, (ii) Syntax Analyzer Design and development, (iii) Semantic Analyzer Design and Development, (iv) Integration of Compiler, (v) Simple GUI development, and (vi) Help Documentation. Among these six modules, we cannot exactly assign a progressive increase of difficulty level or complexity. In fact the first module may be more complex to a student. Further, once he completes the second or third modules, the rest of the modules in the course are likely to be a smooth affair. Such track modules where the difficulty levels of the modules do not follow a progressive increase, are examples of modules of variable (non-progressive) difficulty levels.

4.5 Summary

This chapter covered the essentialities of modularity of activities of the tracks in MT2 method. Modularity provides easiness, simplicity, and effectiveness in not only conducting the activities planned as part of a track, but also introduces flexibility as well as appropriateness in evaluation. The chapter discussed the tradeoff between various choices in modularity such as synchrony (synchronous, semi-synchronous, or asynchronous), size of the modules (larger Vs small modules), and the impact of the number of modules in each track. Difficulty level of the modules is another major factor that needs to be considered. Further, progression of difficulty levels during the course evolution also plays a major role in the effectiveness of the modules.

Be the change you want to see in the world.
- Mahatma Gandhi.

Chapter 5
MT2 Method and UG Research

Dream is not that which you see while sleeping. It is something that does not let you sleep.

-Dr. A. P. J. Abdul Kalam,
President of India (2002-2007) and Founder Chancellor of IIST Trivandrum, Kerala, India.

Enabling Undergraduate research (UG research) is important for attracting more young talents to academics, research, and industry. One of the important techniques to enable UG research activities is by adopting MT2 method at certain specific levels of the UG curriculum. Many premier institutions across the world and some in India, including IITs and IIST Trivandrum, have successfully introduced UG research in an unparalleled manner. This chapter explores the possibilities, in using MT2 method, towards achieving UG research in a university.

5.1 When to Begin Use of MT2 in UG Curriculum?

There are four ways of using MT2 in UG curriculum: (i) Senior UG Elective Courses, (ii) Senior Design Project Courses, (iii) Junior Elective Courses, and (iv) Selected Sophomore[1] Courses.

Senior UG elective courses are the most preferred possibilities to use MT2 method for enhanced UG research in universities. Elective courses are usually specialized courses on a specific area that a student may choose to undertake. Some universities offer honor courses or minor courses that are also considered as elective courses as far as MT2 method is concerned. It is possible to have certain credits assigned to the tracks within a course that follows MT2 method. For example, in a three credit senior elective course, having three tracks, it is possible to have one credit each for the three tracks if the instructor feels appropriate to do so. In the event that the Tracks-2 and -3 are lightweight tracks, then it is also fair to assign two credits to the Track-1 (Lecture track) and assign half credits each to the Tracks-2 and -3.

Consider a hypothetical engineering senior elective course for *Spacecraft Engineering*. It is possible to allocate the credits as per the following distribution: (i) Track-1 can be a lecture track where the design and engineering aspects of spacecraft development will be covered with one credit, (ii) Track-2 can consist of activities leading to the development of a spacecraft such as a nano-satellite which may be assigned another credit, and (iii) Track-3 can be utilized for the documentation of the activities and designs carried out in Track-2 with a credit value of one credit. Therefore, a three track MT2 approach can be utilized for such a Spacecraft Engineering course at senior elective UG level.

Another opportunity for using MT2 method for UG research is in Engineering Design Projects that are specialized courses designed to provide a student exposure to the world of design by carrying out a project in an industry or academic department. When applying MT2 method in such Engineering Design courses, it should be made clear that the smaller fraction of the credits shall be assigned to the lecture track. That is, a substantial faction of the overall course credits shall be assigned to the design activity related tracks. Let us consider one example similar to the course ECE 191 existing in the Electrical and Computer Engineering Department of University of California San Diego, San Diego, CA 92093. The ECE 191 course does not use MT2 method currently. One way to use MT2 method is to define three tracks where the Track-1 (Lecture track) can be assigned about one third of the total credits. The rest of the two thirds of the credits shall be considered for the Tracks-2 and -3. Tracks-2 and -3, respectively, could be defined, as an example, as (i) Design, Development, and Qualification, and (ii) Documentation. Since the Track-2 here is the most challenging track, making it eligible for a higher fraction of the credits is natural and just.

Similar to the Senior UG Elective Courses and Senior Engineering Design Courses, MT2 method can also be applied for Junior Elective Courses and selected Sophomore Courses where specialized knowledge levels are expected from students. However, sufficient care shall be taken for determining Junior or Sophomore course to be considered suitable for applying MT2 method. MT2 method can be applied for carefully identified courses where the depth of knowledge as well as specialization is required. Optional, minor, honor, or elective courses at Junior or Sophomore years are most suitable. Instructor may approach the university to get a prior approval in practicing MT2 at junior levels so that the execution of the course can be easier.

5.2 How to Use MT2 Method in UG Curriculum?

Once the courses are identified where MT2 method can be adopted, some preparations are necessary to be carried out by the instructor. Instructor shall identify the following: (i) size of the class in terms of the number of students who are crediting the course, (ii) availability of sufficient number of Teaching Assistants or junior/contract teachers to help conduct the class, (iii) internal training for the Teaching Assistants and Junior/Contract teachers about the course, (iv) preparation of logistics plan for the evaluation process, and (v) mid-course review and improvement process.

One of the biggest problems universities face is the management of UG classes. UG classes are usually large classes where many classes have already swelled to more than 150 students across the world's best universities. Some universities such as IIT Kharagpur, India, where UG classes have crossed even 200 students. The average class size in University of California San Diego, San Diego, CA, USA, is above 55 when averaged across classes of all sizes [13]. Further, the public universities across the world are under pressure to increase the enrollment due to the growing college-going population as well as shortage of university admission seats. Such kind of growth of class sizes due to high enrollment is increasingly present in the developing world. Therefore, when employing MT2 method in such large UG classes, an instructor has to make some additional preparations in comparison to the Masters classes. Therefore, estimating the size of the class where the instructor is planning to apply MT2 is important for assessing the requirements.

Once the class size is estimated, the instructor shall evaluate the requirement of assistance in terms of teaching assistants, junior teachers, or contract teachers who assist the main faculty/instructor for a course. Based on MT2 requirements, for every 15 students beyond the base class strength of 20, one teaching assistant is needed. In the case of junior/contract teachers, one teacher per 20 students may be assigned to support the main course instructor.

Assume a large class of 100 UG students, where an instructor is able to assemble a team including himself and four TAs. It is important to provide sufficient training/instructions to the TAs such that they understand MT2 method clearly and effectively so that they will be able to assist the class properly. In order to communicate the plan of the tracks, modules of the tracks, evaluation processes, as well as the support required from the TAs, the instructor shall conduct a special orientation session for the TAs. The orientation session shall communicate the details so that the TAs may prepare in advance for the sessions. In addition to the orientation session at the beginning of the course, periodic informal reviews shall be conducted on how the TAs perform with their assistance to the instructor. Instructor may also make necessary training sessions for TAs if they need help with the process of assistance. In the case of junior/contract teachers who are recruited for helping an instructor with a specific course, they may also need similar orientation as well as mid-course training to effectively assist the course instructor. The amount of involvement required for training them is likely to be less than that is needed for TAs in most universities because junior/contract teachers are paid for full time effort in such activities.

Training of evaluation logistics and the method of evaluation of modules need special attention in cases where TAs or junior/contract teachers are assigned to help an instructor in the conduct of a course as per MT2 method. It is important that the instructor must specifically address the evaluation methods, important points, and expectations for each module completed by the students within the tracks of the course. In some cases, demonstrations of functional models, reports of studies, proof of theorems, results of simulations, results of experiments, or compiling data can be methods of evaluation of the modules within the tracks. It is also possible to rotate the TAs or junior/contact teachers to various sections of the students of the class so that the students get an averaged quality support from all the TAs or junior/contract teachers.

The instructor who undertakes MT2 method for UG programs shall constantly monitor the progress of the tracks as well as delivery of modules in order to ensure the success of the course. It is also important for making mid-course corrections or adaptations of the modules so that the tasks can be completed within a stipulated time. In some cases, the completion of a certain module may require a specific set of data that may be unavailable. Instructor may make alternative datasets available so that the students can progress in their task execution of modules. Therefore, periodic mid-course review and improvisation shall be conducted by the instructor throughout the course.

5.3 What to Expect in the Use of MT2 Method in UG Curriculum?

Universities that adopt MT2 method for UG courses according to the methods mentioned earlier in this chapter, receive many benefits ranging from the better learning, high professional quality, research-readiness, and above all substantially good employability of the students.

The main benefit of employing MT2 method for UG curriculum is better learning. Since MT2 method provides multiple modalities through the use of various tracks, a student learns better than the traditional academic courses where the learning is mostly based on lecturing. Activity tracks and their realization in modules provide a student better grasping capability on a subject.

The professional quality that can be expected from the use of MT2 method in UG students is better than the traditional academic programs. Since the tracks mostly involve activities surrounding the lectures, students receive much more professional understanding about the subject of study.

The most important benefit of UG research enabled by MT2 method is the enhanced research-readiness of the graduates taking the program. Since research skills are important in most high-tech industries, obtaining a large population of research-ingrained graduates is very challenging. However, since the introduction of MT2 with research and experiments tracks can inculcate research oriented learning, thereby, resulting in highly research-ready graduates. Finally, the use of MT2 in UG research enhances employability of graduates. The multi-modal learning provides students deeper and practical awareness of various topics covered in such a course, the employability is enhanced.

In conclusion, MT2 method can benefit the UG education in various ways including deeper learning, better professional quality, high research-readiness, and increased employability of graduates.

5.4 Summary

This chapter discussed how MT2 can be utilized to substantially improve research capabilities of UG students in universities. UG research becomes an important objective of all universities due to the enormous benefits it gives to the student population. MT2 method can be used to enable UG research in most university curriculum.

Education is not the learning of facts, but the training of the mind to think.
- Albert Einstein.

Chapter 6
Teaching Philosophies and Productivity Tools

Education is the kindling of a flame, not the filling of a vessel.
- Socrates, Greek philosopher.

6.1 Introduction

Ever since the cognitive evolution of homo-sapiens, the ability to teach and learn has started taking an important role among human beings. In the case of hunting skills, war-craft, agricultural skills, or even in all matters related to survival, teaching has played an important role in the evolution as well as transfer of knowledge from one human to another. *"Teaching philosophy refers to the consolidated philosophical statement about the concept, ideas, and underlying principles of teaching and learning in a human community."* The well-defined and recognizable human philosophy of teaching is as old as at least 5000 years. The oldest established universities were as old as 300 BCE. In this chapter, some of the well known teaching philosophies from various regions of the world are presented in brief. Further, some of the important tools and resources essential for improving productivity and efficiency of teachers and students are provided.

6.2 Reward of a Teacher

Recently, one of my former students, Ms. Archana C. M., asked me to participate in a video interview that she had been coordinating about teaching, philosophy of teaching, and best practices in teaching as well as other matters such as work-life balance. During the interview, the matter about the preparations needed for a class lecture came to our discussion. I responded to her that the *biggest reward of a teacher is nothing but the glow in the eyes of a student who receive an excellent class.* I strongly believe that despite the occupation as a teacher, salary received for teaching, and the teacher's own interest in teaching, my reward of teaching is the glow in the eyes of my students.

Students become very happy with a teacher only when they clearly understand the subject taught by the teacher. Therefore, preparation for the class lectures is very important. To make sure I provide a good class, I prepare many hours before beginning a new topic that I had not taught before. For the lectures that I had taught *a priori,* my preparation time is substantially less. For a faculty who is interested in receiving the reward, the best advice I provide is: *Rehearse the lecture well, before you step in to the lecture hall.*

6.3 Why Teaching is Effective for Modern Human Beings?

It is important to understand why teaching and learning or any kind of skill training is very effective for the evolved human compared to other animals. Dr. V. S. Ramachandran [15], Professor at the Department of Psychology and Neurosciences, University of California San Diego, San Diego, has studied the motor neurons and mirror motor neurons and revealed the impact of them in human evolution. Motor neurons are a group of special neurons located in the front of the human brains and are found to be active when a person utilizes his muscles for various physical activities such as taking a book in hand, throwing a basket ball, or kicking a soccer ball. In other words, the necessary sequence of signals, to operate the muscles, are produced by the motor neurons. Any damage to the motor neurons or the nerves that carry signals from motor neurons to the muscles can leave the person disabled as well as his muscles atrophied. The fine motor skills necessary for some of the professionals such as surgeons, musicians, artists, or sportsmen are typically accomplished by the training of a person over a long period of time. Long duration training helps the proper networking of neurons in one's brain in such a way to accomplish the fine motor skills.

More interesting and valuable are the mirror motor neurons when human evolution by education and training is concerned. Mirror motor neurons are a small group of motor neurons that gets activated when a person sees an action performed by another person. That means, when a teacher performs an experiment by physically moving an experimental device in the class, the students get a feeling of the experiment as if the experiment is being conducted by them. The activation of motor mirror neurons help them to conduct the physical activity effortlessly by the students. Most of the human-developed education and training systems utilize the capabilities of motor mirror neurons. Development of culture, civilization, use of equipments, training physical skills by a coach, learning lessons through visual observation, and many other such transfer of knowledge happen through the use of mirror motor neurons. Therefore, teaching and learning are very effective due to the presence of mirror motor neurons in human brains.

6.4 Future of Teaching

Future of teaching is an open question in today's world of rapid technology evolution. Receiving knowledge and wisdom from the face of a teacher has been the only way for becoming knowledgeable in the past. Evolution of large number of books helped people to understand by reading them. New technologies such as Internet further advanced the knowledge base as well as the acquisition of knowledge through the use of a computer. Today, as we face the development of artificial intelligence driven technology, we are at cross roads on how the acquisition of knowledge will be advanced by the use of artificial intelligence. Massive Open Online Courseware (MOOC) technologies helped advance the class room sizes to very large sizes to even millions of students per course. On top of all the above innovations in education and training, the future takes a huge leap and directional change with the advent of technologies such as tactile Internet [32], Neuralink [27], as well as automation.

Tactile Internet [32] helps effect human presence remotely through the very high speed, ultra low latency, and very high reliability Internet. Another example is a robotic surgeon carrying out a surgery remotely even from another continent. Tactile Internet services may include teaching, education, and skill training areas in the near future. Class rooms will be virtual with students attending from all around the world. Class rooms of very large size can be accomplished through the combination of virtual reality, augmented reality, artificial intelligence, and Tactile Internet.

Neuralink [27] is a company established by Elon Musk[1] in order to develop neuro-technology solutions such as high speed brain-to-machine interface. Traditionally, brain received information to be processed and stored over the five sensory inputs, touch, smell, taste, vision, and hearing. These inputs were processed and stored in the form of a certain network topology among the neurons in the human brain. Neuralink develops a direct communication link between computers and human brain so that information storage, processing, and retrieval can be transformed significantly.

Over the human brain interfaces created by Neuralink's technology, knowledge transfer, education, training, and radical computer-aided education of various physical systems can be accomplished. Neuralink technology, once developed in full end-to-end application system, can transform teaching-learning processes by providing accelerated, automated, and augmented learning mechanisms. Therefore, human-driven education and training may face slow and steady obsolescence in the future.

6.5 Glimpses of Teaching Philosophies Around the World

Teaching and learning philosophies differ in various parts of the world. Traditional Indian philosophy enforces a set of very important behavioral aspects to the students' interaction with the teachers (Gurus[2]). In Indian subcontinent, teaching philosophy was revolving about dedication to the Guru's sayings as well as to the Guru and his family.

On the other hand, the Greek or Western teaching philosophies do not demand much loyalty from the students to the teachers. Younger religions such as Islam provide as much preference as possible to teaching and learning as the oldest Indian teaching philosophy. A brief description of various socio-cultural-religious treatments on teaching and learning is provided here.

6.5.1 Traditional Indian Teaching Philosophy

India was known as the land of knowledge and wisdom before the industrial revolution. India had established some of the best and largest universities, in Nalanda and Takshashila, where students and scholars from around the world arrived to acquire vedic and traditional knowledge.

One of the important aspects of Indian teaching philosophy is the complete dedication of the student to his Guru (teacher) and Guru's family. In return for the holistic knowledge, the student shall be respectful to the teacher. In most cases, a student is expected to live with the family of the Guru and take care of the household with utmost perfection. Further, students are expected to follow a very complicated and restricted lifestyle. On completion of the education process which usually lasts for several years, a teacher must be given a *Guru Dakshina* which is equivalent to a symbolic fee paid to the teacher.

6.5.2 Chinese Teaching Philosophy

Most notable among all Chinese philosophers who contributed to the development of teaching and education in China is Kong Qui (also known as K'ung Fu-tzu), who is well known to the rest of the world as Confucius (551 BC to 479 BC). His school of thought is now known as Confucianism. Most of his lifetime as a teacher, he worked with a large number of students and left a following who believed in his ideals for a good society. Confucianism followed four books and five classics. While these are not entirely written by Confucius, as there were contributions from his disciples, they remain at the core of Confucianism. The four books are: (i) *Book of Great Learning* which dealt with Chinese political thinking as well as philosophy and remained as the most influential book in both modern and classical Chinese thought, (ii) *Book of Doctrine of the Mean* that dealt with the ways towards accomplishing virtues as defined by Confucius, applicable to all the levels of the society through gentle or golden ways, (iii) *The Analects* that consisted of speeches of Confucius that dealt with the values, morality, and philosophy to be followed by the society, and (iv) *Mencius*, a collection of discussions between the philosopher Mencius and the kings of those times. On the other hand, the five classics are: (i) *The Poetry Classic*, (ii) *The*

Documents Book, (iii) *The Rites Book,* (iv) *The Changes Book*, and (v) *The Spring and Autumn Annals.*

Many of these books and classics included contributions by many others who lived during his time or prior to that. However, Confucius contributed in taking them into the shape and spreading the ideas and philosophical thought in a concise and organized manner. Chinese society, education system, moral values, and public servants are most influenced by the contributions of Confucius even today.

Confucianism dealt with the relationship between teachers and students as well. He developed many thousands of students during his lifetime. His ideals for teaching philosophy included that the teachers to be patient and adapting the methods of teaching to suit the needs of students. Teachers are expected to make significant sacrifice of their time and resources to develop students. Chinese education system demanded students to be loyal, dedicate, honest, as well as humble. Violations of any of these principles are highly resisted by the entire social system including the parents and teachers.

6.5.3 Western Teaching Philosophy

One of the earliest philosophers who contributed to the novel methods of teaching is Plato (423-347 BC[3]) who wrote the famous book *The Republic* as well as established the first Western institution of higher learning, *The Academy*, in ancient Greece. Socrates, teacher of Plato, and Aristotle, leading disciple of Plato, along with Plato made substantial contributions to the development of teaching, education, justice, governance, and excellence in profession. Modern education is rooted on their school of thought. Plato believed in education as a means to accomplish justice that indirectly translates to excellence in work.

6.5.4 Judaic Teaching Philosophy

Jews, known as *People of the Book* in the Middle East, value education and teaching. They believed in passing the fundamental principles of ethics, values, morals, and praying to God as part of their early education. The Old

Testament, the first part of the Bible, stands the testimony to the teaching philosophy of Jews. The main objective of the Torah Study, "study of the religious texts," is aimed at the cultural transfer of religious values and principles to new generation Jews. Jewish religious texts defined the age of starting formal education at around 5-6 years of a child. Further, at every regular interval of 3-5 years of age, appropriate higher levels of religious texts were suggested for teaching. Most importantly, Jewish education philosophy largely advocated avoiding the use of negative reinforcement techniques such as beating or use of cane on younger children by their teachers or elders. Teaching and education, of religious or other knowledge, were given utmost importance in Judaic education philosophy.

6.5.5 Buddhist Teaching Philosophy

Buddhism emerged in the ancient India in 5th century BCE based on the teachings of Gouthama Buddha. Buddhism is rooted on Indian vedic concepts with substantial improvements made on the rituals. One of the main tenants of Gouthama Budda's teaching is that education is meant for attaining the *perfect ultimate wisdom.* In fact, most aspects of Buddhists' religious practice is aimed at achieving the perfect ultimate wisdom. Every child, according to Buddhism, is educated with the objective of raising him as a free, wise, intelligent, moral, secular, and above all non-violent human being. One of the primary philosophies of education is to remove suffering through education as human suffering was caused by lack of knowledge. Since Buddhism does not propagate the concept of super natural forces and their worshipping for removal of suffering, Buddhist philosophy matches the most with the modern research oriented education system. Buddhist philosophy advocates delivery of knowledge through education in democratic and peaceful environments of monasteries of Buddhist temples. Similar to Hinduism-driven Indian education philosophy, many restrictions were attached to students during their student-life. Buddhism, therefore, advocates a philosophy of education where moral, ethical, and human values are taught with an objective to attain human wisdom.

6.5.6 Islamic Teaching Philosophy

Islam provides high preference to teaching and learning. It is recorded by many Islamic texts that one of the very first messages received by Prophet

Muhammad from Allah is about the importance of teaching, reading, and writing. In one of the most decisive wars of Islamic history, the Battle of Badr, Prophet Muhammad and his followers faced the huge army of Quraish of Mecca at Badr, a place closer to Medina. In the bloody battle of Badr, Prophet Muhammad and his followers won. Among the large number of imprisoned enemies, those who could teach and educate Muhammad's followers were pardoned. The Koran underlines the importance of teaching, learning, and acquiring knowledge. The recent high growth of Islam in the western countries is mainly attributed to the religious teaching as well as engagement of children at religious education from a very young age. Islam, therefore, provides high significance to teaching and learning process.

6.6 My Teaching Philosophy and Motivation for MT2 Method

The main motivation behind using the multi-track modular teaching method is to provide a deeper and complete learning of an academic course or a topic under training, through multiple modalities of teaching-learning process. Taking every training course, academic or not, requires investment in terms of time and effort from both the instructors as well as students, therefore, effective learning is important to benefit from the effort put in by the stake-holders.

My teaching philosophy is shaped by experiences dated from my primary school days to my teaching job as a Lecturer at University of California San Diego and my current job as Professor and Head of Department of Avionics, IIST. As the student coordinator of science club at my upper primary school, I was assigned the task of holding weekly science events which involved conducting science quizzes, organizing discussions on scientists and their scientific inventions, and conducting small scientific experiments. As a quiz-master at those weekly science quiz sessions held on Friday afternoons, I used to prepare sets of questions for measuring the scientific awareness among my then peers. Soon I realized the essential methods to prepare the right mix of easy and challenging questions that would both encourage and challenge the rest of the student folks in my upper primary school. During those days, I learned the most important lesson that any teacher in the world would ever need which is nothing but developing the right questions and their sequence that can facilitate learning.

Later during my undergraduate days, I learned another important lesson of teaching; a great teacher must have a clear idea about his students and their knowledge background. Some of my teachers focused their lectures targeting the intellectual levels of select top students in the class and, as a result, half the class could not understand what I was able to understand then. Therefore, delivering the information needs supplementary examples, exercises, or both which need to be fine crafted to suit the spectrum of the knowledge background of the class. In fact, top quality students need less help from their teachers. Many top students are good self learners. A teacher's main contribution is in elevating an average student to become an expert on the topic. I have known several professors who intend to take only very high caliber students for PhD programs. Even in IIST, I could see many such professors. I believe that a brilliant student does not critically require help of a teacher. In fact, a brilliant student may have his own research plans that may not require any meaningful mentoring. On the other hand, I always believe in getting any available student and mentor them to possible higher levels through the mentoring process. I also closely observed, identified, and brought to my own use the approaches practiced by the best teachers among those who taught me during undergraduate and graduate studies. One example best practice that I adopted from my teachers is that a set of carefully chosen supplementary exercises and examples can greatly enhance understanding, especially in the higher education areas such as Computer Science and Engineering.

During my work as a lecturer at UCSD, I provided my Data Networking students with experimental exercises which greatly helped my students connect their theoretical fundamentals with the reality of application. Their interest in my way of teaching was evident even after the completion of that course where some of them stayed back with me for summer projects when the university was closed for holidays. For the course that I taught at UCSD, DATA NETWORKS II, my class was rated at 89% which was the highest ever for that course till then. As a teacher of Computer Networking, I was extremely delighted to see that many students turned back to me in order to receive helpful suggestions on decisions for choosing either appropriate higher studies or a career in industry. Many of these students acted as helpful points of contact in several industries in San Diego, California, during my stay in USA.

I derived significant mentoring experience during my Masters and PhD when I was asked to assist teachers, substitute some of the class hours of teachers, or assist them in laboratory experiments/evaluations. In addition, I had also derived significant research mentoring experience while helping junior students doing their Masters and Bachelors in the High Performance Computing and Networking Laboratory of Indian Institute of Technology Madras, India. Some of the important principles that I understood during those days serve the key pillars of my teaching philosophy: (i) teaching is a holy profession, (ii) feedback is inevitable for teaching, (iii) teaching is a mutual learning process, (iv) multi-modal teaching-learning process is natural.

6.6.1 Teaching is a Holy Profession

First, it is important for a teacher to identify the value of his profession than just to consider it as mere employment. A great teacher can influence his students in such a way that he can build a student community that believes in his vision, ideology, principles, and thought, thereby, making his contribution in the evolution of civilization rememberable for generations. Therefore, my primary philosophy is that *teaching is the holiest of professions.* In order to achieve such great levels of teaching, a teacher must be dedicated, passionate, and sincere to his student folk. A dedicated and knowledgeable teacher can evoke enough passion and zeal among students toward the area of study.

6.6.2 Feedback is Inevitable for Teaching

My second philosophy of teaching is based on my understanding that feedback is essential for an effective teacher. Feedback is a process of a teacher getting a sense of how the students understand a topic that he/she has been teaching in a class/course. Some of the methodologies that can obtain the right feedback are the following: (i) expressions, body languages, and attitude of students in the classroom, (ii) verbal feedback from students such as queries and doubts raised, and discussions during office hours, (iii) performance of students in tests, projects, assignments, and examinations, and (iv) feedback from formal systems such as faculty evaluations. A teacher must have the capability to observe and understand the various modalities of feedback that his/her students give. My teaching methodologies follow an adaptive strategy that fine tunes the teaching process based on the continuous feedback obtained from the above mentioned feedback methodologies. Feedback, therefore, is inevitable for effective teaching.

6.6.3 Teaching is a Mutual Learning Process

Students as well as teachers learn together! "Teaching is a mutual learning process" is the third important teaching principle that I believe in. It is a fact that learning is a mutual activity and, therefore, in order to improve the knowledge levels in the forefront of science and technology areas, it is essential to incorporate new and unsolved areas of study into the curriculum. It is possible to see that early solutions for hard core problems may emerge out of class room discussions and, therefore, historically unsolved problems may be suggested for class room discussions. For example, computer networking is both a theoretical and an applied research field where it is essential to learn the theoretical concepts and analytical approaches in order to apply them for developing new computer networking systems or to analyze complex existing systems. Answering the "How?" and "Why?" of every stage of students' learning is essential in addition to just knowing "What?" Such an approach will foster the independent thinking, especially for hard core problem solving applications. Therefore, once the class is informally ranked based on students' knowledge background, my approach is to answer questions from the weaker students and always pose questions to the most knowledgeable students. Such presentation of important questions to the class especially on the unsolved problems in computer networking prompts intellectually stimulating arguments which in many cases in the past led to meaningful solutions. A similar experience occurred when I co-advised the ECE191 Engineering Design Project at University of California San Diego. During the initial stages of the project, I had led the student group in its "baby steps" in the area of wireless networking, medium access control protocols, and wireless mesh networks. After a few weeks into the project, our discussions on "Why?" and "How?" on every step enabled my students to innovate and explore new areas on designing MAC protocols which can increase the network capacity in wireless mesh networks. Such solutions are possible only due to the logical thinking capability derived from the "teaching-the-learning" process than just teaching a subject.

6.6.4 Multi-modal Teaching-learning Process is Natural

I very often find the use of visualization tools handy for explaining complex concepts which require help of graphical content. On the other hand, a large fraction of the student population finds that slide presentations based on commercial software such as Microsoft Powerpoint, Apple Keynote, and other software tools tend to contribute to an increased speed of lecturing, thereby, limiting the students' learning ability. Not only that, in many cases, based on the students' feedback, I noticed that a mix of multiple tools is necessary for conducting a good class. For example, the primary media of presentation must be a form of handwriting medium such as black board and white chalk with complementary visualization tools reserved only for elucidating complex concepts. For example, for Computer Networking education, numerous software tools can be used for more effective learning. Some of such tools that are useful for wireless networking courses include the wireless traffic monitoring tools such as Wireshark (formerly Ethereal) [35], The Jupyter Notebook (formerly known as ipython) [21], and CommView [5]. Additional tools can be used within a class room or lab are simulator tools such as Network Simulator-2 [26], NAM [25], OPNET [28], MATLAB [22], QualNet [29], Urban DTN Simulator [34], and NetSim [24].

Simulators and other tools can help in delivering and clarifying information on some of the extremely complex concepts in Computer Networking. In my experiments with Data Networking students at UCSD, I had extensively used Wireshark, MATLAB, network simulators, and real-world wireless network devices such as routers which were appreciated by the student community. Ideally, what I typically use is to supplement every three or four credit theoretical course with a one or two credit hands-on component or a laboratory course. During the laboratory course, the instructor may provide a set of experiments which can be used for concretizing the fundamentals learned in the theoretical course. MT2 method is an extension of the concept of adding laboratory components to an academic course in a much more enriched and effective multi-modal teaching approach.

6.7 Tools for Improving Teaching-Learning Process

The identification of the right tools is important for accomplishing success in any activity. For a student, the intention for learning is the first and foremost tool required for making an improvement. Developing that positive intention is typically accomplished by most students. What is missing in most students is the right set of tools to maintain that intention. Here, some of the tools used by great men of wisdom are described for the benefit of students. Examples of such tools are: (i) Cornell note-taking method, (ii) Franklin's chart, (iii) Eisenhower's matrix, and (iv) the Three Bins technique for task prioritization.

6.7.1 Cornell Note-taking Method

Taking short notes during lectures or talks is essential to remember and benefit from the topics discussed in them. Cornell note-taking method provides a better approach to taking notes. As per Cornell note-taking method, the page of the notebook/notepad is marked in to the following four areas as shown in Figure 6.1: (i) Title area, (ii) Main note-taking area, (iii) Cue column area, and (iv) Summary area.

The upper area is designated as the title area where the title of the course, the course code, instructor's name, class number, topic number, date, and time are noted down. The information in the title may be noted down during or after the class. Since, there likely are many classes, in a day, it is important to do it before a student forgets to note it down.

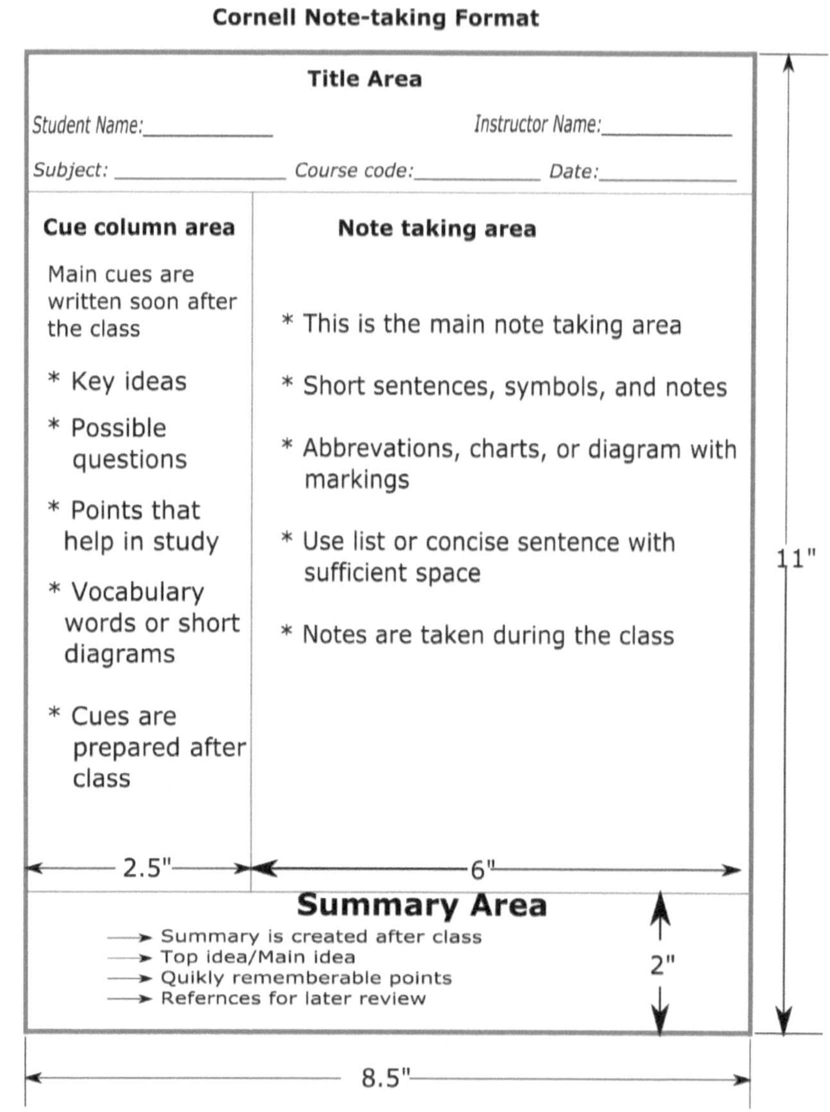

Figure 6.1: Example of Page Format for Cornell Note-taking Method.

The second area is the main note-taking area where the main notes are taken. Short sentences, symbols, abbreviations, charts, diagrams, markings, lists, and bulleted points, are noted down in this area during the lecture. Since taking notes is done in a quick manner, it is important to leave gaps between the lines so that the user may fill it in later when he/she gets time.

The vertical column area, marked the Cue column area with approximate 2.5 inch width, is meant for filling, the main cues after the class. This column area provides important cues, for preparing for the examinations, with key ideas, possible questions, points that help in studying further, vocabulary words, short diagrams, or other points useful for review and study.

The bottom area, marked as Summary area, with approximate height 2 inch is meant to be filled after class with a brief summary of the notes taken in the above mentioned Note taking area. A brief summary including the main ideas, quickly rememberable points, and references for later review are examples of the information to be written down for the Summary area. The Summary area helps in quickly passing through the entire class in a much shorter time.

6.7.2 Benjamin Franklin's Chart for Better Habits

Benjamin Franklin was a legendary figure of the United States of America who became an accomplished diplomat, celebrated scientist, pioneering publisher, inventor of many apparatuses, man of letters, and above all a fine human being. He developed and practiced a chart-based method for developing good habits or virtues. He identified 13 habits/virtues, based on his knowledge and experience, which are of importance for a human being and prepared weekly charts to mark the occurrence of violation of the practices of those virtues. The charts, marked with number of days of a week where violations of the virtues happened, provide a feedback to the user, thereby; tendency to stop repeating them develops. The 13 virtues suggested by Benjamin Franklin in his biography [36] are as follows:

1. **Temperance:** Eat not to dullness; drink not to elevation.
2. **Silence:** Speak not but what may benefit others or yourself; avoid trifling conversation.
3. **Order:** Let all your things have their places; let each part of your business have its time.
4. **Resolution:** Resolve to perform what you ought; perform without fail what you resolve.

5. **Frugality:** Make no expense but to do good to others or yourself; i.e., waste nothing.
6. **Industry:** Lose no time; be always employ'd in something useful; cut off all unnecessary actions.
7. **Sincerity:** Use no hurtful deceit; think innocently and justly, and, if you speak, speak accordingly.
8. **Justice:** Wrong none by doing injuries, or omitting the benefits that are your duty.
9. **Moderation:** Avoid extremes; forbear resenting injuries so much as you think they deserve.
10. **Cleanliness:** Tolerate no uncleanliness in body, cloaths, or habitation.
11. **Tranquillity:** Be not disturbed at trifles, or at accidents common or unavoidable.
12. **Chastity:** Rarely use venery but for health or offspring, never to dullness, weakness, or the injury of your own or another's peace or reputation.
13. **Humility:** Imitate great people such as Jesus and Socrates.

The last virtue can be slightly modified with examples to reflect on the contemporary world as follows:

Humility: *Imitate great people such as Socrates of Greece, Confucius of China, Benjamin Franklin of USA, Abraham Lincoln of USA, Mahatma Gandhi of India, Martin Luther King of USA, and Nelson Mandela of South Africa, and take lessons from Religious figures such as Moses, Lord Srikrishna, Jesus Christ of Nazareth, Gouthama Buddha of Indian subcontinent, and Prophet Muhammad of Arabia.*

Even though the virtues mentioned above are worthy to be habituated, it is very challenging to maintain them as a habit for any student. Franklin created the chart-based approach where he created columns for the habits for each day of a week. Further, he focused on developing the habits one after the other because accomplishing all the habits together is difficult. In the first several weeks, he considers an attempt to create a habit only for one virtue.

Example of Franklin's chart for the first virtue "Temperance"

Temperance: Eat not to dullness; Drink not to elevation.						
Monday	Tuesday	Wednesday	Thursday	Friday	Sarturday	Sunday
*				*		*

Figure 6.2: Example of Franklin's Chart for one virtue for a period of one week.

For example, for the first week, he focused only on one virtue, **Temperance**. Any day he observed himself at fault in the virtue, he black-marked the day in the chart (Figure 6.2). Over the next several weeks, once he mastered the first virtue, *Temperance,* then he considered the second virtue, *Silence*, to the table as the second row item as shown in Figure 6.3. After mastering the first two virtues, the other virtues are added one by one as rows to the chart where he worked to habituate the rest. It is possible for a student to practice the same principle for his/her habit creation.

Example of Franklin's chart for the first two virtues							
Week days / Virtues	Monday	Tuesday	Wednesday	Thursday	Friday	Sarturday	Sunday
Temperance: Eat not to dullness; Drink not to elevation							
Silence: Speak not but what may benefit others or yourself; Avoid trifling conversation	*				*		*

Figure 6.3: Example of Franklin's Chart for Two Virtues for a Period of a Week.

One natural question arises in a reader's mind is why Franklin's chart works for students? My observation about Franklin's chart is that it helps a student to get a feedback on his/her accomplishments about the virtues. The success or failure to practice a habit in a consistent manner provides a very necessary feedback to the student, which can work out miracles in improving the student. I do strongly believe that following the chart can help a student immensely to look inward and refine to such a level that academic accomplishments can become easier. A chart with all the virtues marked is shown in Figure 6.4.

How to use Franklin's Chart for Today's Students' Needs

The approach used by Franklin in his chart can be used by students in today's environment, where they face challenges with modern virtues, as well. The key difference between the times of Franklin and ours is that there exist a large number of new and inappropriate habits that came into existence in human lives due to the advancement of technology. For example, modern habits of inappropriateness can be watching television programs for long hours, working with mobile computers in a contiguous manner, browsing the Internet for inappropriate content, or addiction to playing computer games. Students with interest in stopping some of their habits, that are counterproductive to their life's goals, can use a modification to the list of virtues that Franklin had utilized. For example, a student who wishes to reduce his/her Internet addiction may create a new virtue "Frugal Use of The Internet: Use the Internet resources frugally, not beyond what is necessary." If a student is interested in minimizing the influence of computer games in his/her life, can consider creating a virtue "Minimal Gaming: Use Computer Games to exercise the brain, not to the extent of getting troubled." An example of the Franklin's chart modified with the two above mentioned virtues is shown in Figure 6.5.

Example of Franklin's Chart for all the virtues

Weekdays / Virtues	Monday	Tuesday	Wednesday	Thursday	Friday	Saturday	Sunday
Temperence							
Silence							
Order							
Resolution							
Frugality							
Industry							
Sincerity							
Justice							
Moderation							
Cleanliness							
Traquility							
Chastity							
Humility			*	*	*		

Figure 6.4: Example of Franklin's Chart for all the Virtues

Figure 6.5 answers one of the important questions on how to use Franklin's chart for today's needs of students for developing better habits or removing inappropriate habits. Student readers are advised to consider creating their own charts for their needed virtues. In conclusion, the Franklin's chart method is a self-feedback based method for creating and sustaining virtues in students.

Example of Franklin's chart modified with two modern virtues							
Week days / Virtues	Monday	Tuesday	Wednesday	Thursday	Friday	Sarturday	Sunday
Frugal Use of The Internet: Use the Internet resources frugally, not beyond what is necessary.		*		*			
Minimal Gaming: Use Computer Games to exercise the brain, not to the extend of getting troubled.	*				*		*

Figure 6.5: Example of Franklin's Chart Modified with two Modern Virtues

6.7.3 Eisenhower's Matrix

The *Eisenhower's Matrix* or *Eisenhower Method* was popularized by the American Army general turned President Dwight D. Eisenhower [10]. Eisenhower was the 34th American President whose presidency spanned the term 1953-1961. He was a trained military leader and known for his professional attitude toward problem solving and working at high productivity levels. He is said to have made a famous quote that goes as follows: "What is important is seldom urgent and what is urgent is seldom important." The difference between urgent and important matters is of significant interest for the discussion here. Important matters are truly important to oneself such as those that contribute to his/her long-term objectives or goals, steps needed for one's long-term accomplishments, or even the mission in one's life. On the other hand, the urgent or time-sensitive matters are those that require your immediate response such as responding to a quick fire or an accident. Here, a modified version of

Eisenhower's original matrix, presented for the benefit of teachers, is adapted to suit students as well in the following sections.

According to the Eisenhower's matrix, all tasks, potentially in an officer's or a teacher's work table, can be categorized into the following four areas:

1. Important and Time-sensitive
2. Important and Not Time-sensitive
3. Not important and Time-sensitive
4. Not important and Not Time-sensitive

A 2x2 matrix with two rows and two columns is devised with the above factors such as Time-sensitiveness and Importance, in order for arriving at Teachers' productivity enhancement matrix, as can be seen from Figure 6.6. The first quadrant in the matrix shown in Figure 6.6 consists of the tasks that are of high importance. A user, here a teacher, must focus on these activities immediately. Here the importance is attributed to the benefit of the teachers' professional long-term objectives. The second quadrant (Q2) includes the category of items which are important but not time-sensitive. These are of second priority which shall be done by the teacher with a clear plan or schedule to do them. The third quadrant (Q3) involves tasks that are time-sensitive but not important. Such tasks shall not be delayed, however, a teacher is not required to spent his/her own time to do such tasks because those tasks are not important for himself/herself. Therefore, the teacher may find a suitable alternative person to delegate the Q3 tasks. Doing such unimportant tasks can drain the teacher's time with matters that others can handle better. Finally, the quadrant-4 (Q4) consists of a category of items which are neither important nor time-sensitive. Such tasks can be completely disregarded, deleted, or placed at very low priority in a teacher's task list.

	Time-sensitive	Not Time-sensitive
Important	Q1 Highest priority (Do these tasks immediately.)	Q2 Second highest Priority (Plan, Schedule, and Do these tasks by yourself.)
Not Important	Q3 Third highest Priority (Try delegate to others for immediate action. If not, do it yourself, without much delay.)	Q4 Last priority (Ignore these tasks or give lowest priority.)

Figure 6.6: Eisenhower's Matrix for Teachers' Productivity Enhancement

Q1: Important and Time-sensitive

Examples of the tasks that a teacher faces under the important and time-sensitive category are as follows: evaluation of quizzes, class tests, mid-terms, and finals. Additional such tasks can be: research paper submissions, project proposal or final result submissions, family's urgent matters, or urgent hospital visits.

Q2: Important and Not Time-sensitive

Examples of tasks that fall under the category of important and not time-sensitive are as follows: research paper preparations, project funding proposal preparations, research data collection, research discussions, industry collaboration visits, and periodic health check-up.

Q3: Not Important and Time-sensitive

Some of the example tasks of this category can be as follows: a visitor who turned up without prior appointment, a suddenly scheduled administrative meeting, or an unexpected event requiring quick attention and can be handled better by someone else.

Q4: Not Important and Not Time-sensitive

The Q4 tasks include all tasks other than the tasks of the above mentioned quadrants Q1, Q2, and Q3.

6.7.4 Eisenhower's Matrix Adapted for Students

Figure 6.7 shows an adaptation of Eisenhower's matrix for students' productivity enhancement.

	Time-sensitive	Not Time-sensitive
Important	Q1 Highest priority (Do these tasks immediately.)	Q3 Third highest Priority (Do these tasks on a schedule, by yourself.)
Not Important	Q2 Second highest Priority (Take help of others to complete them without much delay.)	Q4 Lowest Priority (Ignore or delete these tasks, or provide lowest priority.)

Figure 6.7: Eisenhower's Matrix for Students' Productivity Enhancement [Note that the order of the quadrants Q2 and Q3 are swapped between the Teachers' and Students' Matrices].

Unlike teachers, students cannot delegate the authority as they do not have subordinates who can be delegated with work. All the tasks are to be handled by students themselves. Therefore, the priority order changes, from highest priority to lowest, within the matrix in the following sequence: Q1->Q2->Q3->Q4. Note that the locations Q2 and Q3 quadrants have been swapped compared to the teachers' Eisenhower's matrix.

Q1: Important and Time-sensitive

Examples of important and time-sensitive tasks are as follows: class tests, midterms, quizzes, or finals, project submissions, assignment submissions, family's urgent matters, or part-time work-related matters (if any).

Q2: Not Important and Time-sensitive

Some of the examples of important and time-sensitive tasks are as follows: Returning library books or other borrowed items, reporting for duty to a part-time job, or renewal of rental items.

Q3: Important and Not Time-sensitive

Some of the examples of important and not time-sensitive tasks are as follows: preparation of topics for exams that are not scheduled yet, literature survey for research topics, or preparation for future jobs/placement opportunities.

Q4: Not Important and Not Time-sensitive

Under this matrix cell, all matters that are not covered under Q1, Q2, and Q3 above, are placed.

Eisenhower's matrix, in summary, is a very useful productivity enhancement tool for teachers and students for task organization.

6.7.5 Three Bins Technique for Task Prioritization

Many times, when an individual is tasked with multiple tasks, it is important to quickly and effectively complete all the tasks. When I was doing the administrative responsibility of Avionics Department of IIST, I had utilized a method, named as Three Bins technique that uses three conceptual bins to prioritize the tasks that are to be completed. In some cases, when I return from official tours, many papers get piled up for approvals. Most such papers were either pending due to the busy schedule of my work week or piled up during my absence. The Three Bins technique involves two stages of operation and three bins of category of work: Stage-1: Quick overview and classification and Stage-2: Finishing in sequence from the first bin to the third bin.

In Stage-1, all the pending work is quickly reviewed and categorized into three bins (or three categories): Bin-1: work items that require very short time to complete, Bin-2: work items that require medium amount of time to complete, and finally Bin-3: work items that require longer amount of time to complete. That is, the binning decision is made based on the estimate of time required to complete the work. A student or faculty shall quickly assess the time required to complete each work and categorize them among the three bins.

It is important to ensure that the Stage-1 process, task classification, is completed in a short time. It may require certain amount of work experience to effectively carry out the classification in a short time. A new teacher or a new administrator may take a certain moderate amount of time to complete the classification. However, it is important to note that as time progresses, a teacher/administrator is guaranteed to gain sufficient expertise to improve his efficiency in the classification stage.

In Stage-2, the categorized tasks in Bin-1 are taken first for working on them. By taking the items from Bin-1, we accomplish the popular *Shortest-job-first* algorithm, used in Computer Science and Engineering area that is known to produce optimal solutions in completing all the jobs in terms of the lowest average task completion time. That is, our first attendance to the tasks in Bin-1, containing the work items that can be quickly completed, helps us to complete the entire set of tasks in the three bins with lowest average task completion time.

An empirical time estimate for each of the three bins can be used as follows:

- Bin-1: Tasks that require less than or equal to 5 minutes to complete.
- Bin-2: Tasks that require between 5 minutes and 1 hour to complete.
- Bin-3: Tasks that require more than an hour to complete.

Once the pending jobs are classified into the three bins, the tasks identified in the Bin-1 are taken for completion. After finishing the jobs in Bin-1, the rest of the two bins, Bin-2 and Bin-3, can be taken up for completion.

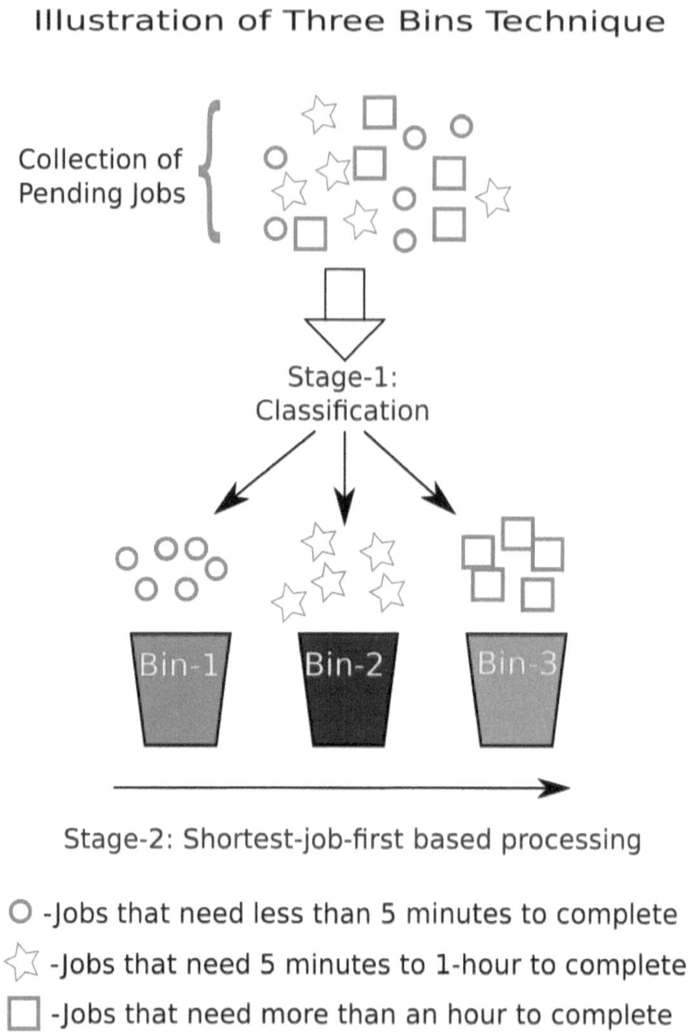

Figure 6.8: An Illustration of Three Bins Technique

Three Bins technique is effective in completing all the jobs with lowest average job completion time. The question is why Three Bins technique is effective?

Why is the Three Bins Technique Effective?

Three Bins technique is effective because it follows the shortest-job-first approach that is proven to be completing the tasks within the lowest average task completion time. Let us consider the following example describing the shortest-job-first approach. There are four pending jobs, J1, J2, J3, J4, and J5, with the time required to complete them, respectively, as 15, 2, 8, 10, and 5 minutes as shown in Table 6.1.

Table 6.1: Example of Five Jobs and their Completion Times.

Job Number	Time Required to Complete (minutes)
J1	15
J2	2
J3	8
J4	10
J5	5

Consider a basic order of J1 through J5 for execution. Figure 6.9 shows the execution completion times of J1, J2, J3, J4, and J5 are, respectively, as follows: 15, 17, 25, 35, and 40 minutes. Therefore, the average completion time of the jobs is obtained as (15+17+25+35+40)/5 = 26.4 minutes as can be seen from Figure 6.9 (a). In the first 15 minutes, only J1 could be completed, thereby, the rest of the four jobs were made to wait.

Now, consider the reordering of the jobs based on the shortest-job-first approach. The reordered job sequence is shown in Figure 6.9 (b). That is, based on the shortest job first, we can find the order of the jobs as J2, J5, J3, J4, and J1. If we proceed with completing the jobs in this sequence, then we can find the completion time for the jobs can be as follows: J2 (completed at 2nd minute), J5 (completed at 7th minute), J3 (completed at 15th minute), J4 (completed at 25th minute) and J1 (completed at 40th minute). Now, the sum of the completion times can be obtained as 2 + 7 + 15 + 25 + 40 = 89 minutes. Therefore, the average completion time for the jobs is 89/5= 17.5 minutes. Comparing with the basic job order (J1, J2, J3, J4, and J5, taking average completion time of 26.4 minutes), on an average, every job in shortest-path-first order needs only lower amount of time (17.5 minutes/job). That is, in the first 15 minutes, three jobs have been completed, thereby, resulting in only two jobs to wait, in comparison to the previous case where four jobs were in waiting during the first 15 minutes.

Note that in either case, the total time to complete the jobs remains at 40 minutes.

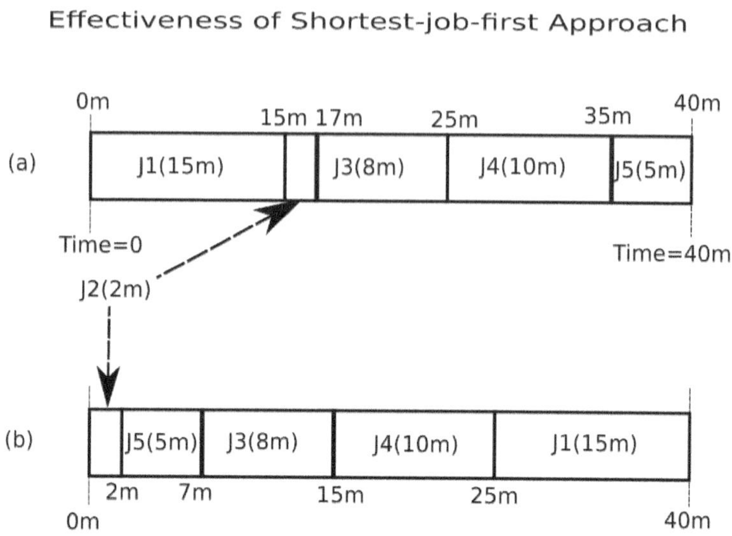

Figure 6.9: Effectiveness of shortest-job-first method

The benefit of task completion based on shortest-job-first approach comes because many short jobs can be completed without waiting for the jobs that need longer duration for completion. The shortest-job-first approach is found to be providing optimal average job completion time in several cases including the above example. A more interesting approach is to combine the Three Bins technique with the Eisenhower's matrix.

Combining the Three Bins Technique on Eisenhower's Matrix

While Eisenhower's matrix helps in classifying the tasks based on the importance as well as time-sensitiveness, it does not provide any idea on how to proceed among the tasks within a matrix cell. The Three Bins technique can be used within each matrix cell to accomplish better handling of the tasks with lowest average job completion time. Consider the following example where one of the cells of the Eisenhower's matrix is containing a few jobs to be completed. Among these jobs, the quick Stage-1 processing can be carried out in order to classify the jobs into the three categories: (i) jobs that require less than 5 minutes, (ii) jobs that require more than 5 minutes and less than an hour for completion, and (iii) jobs that require more than an hour to complete. Once the jobs are organized in to the three bins, the Stage-2 of processing of Three Bins technique can be employed starting with the bin with the shortest job duration. Figure 6.10 illustrates the use of the Three Bins technique in Eisenhower's matrix.

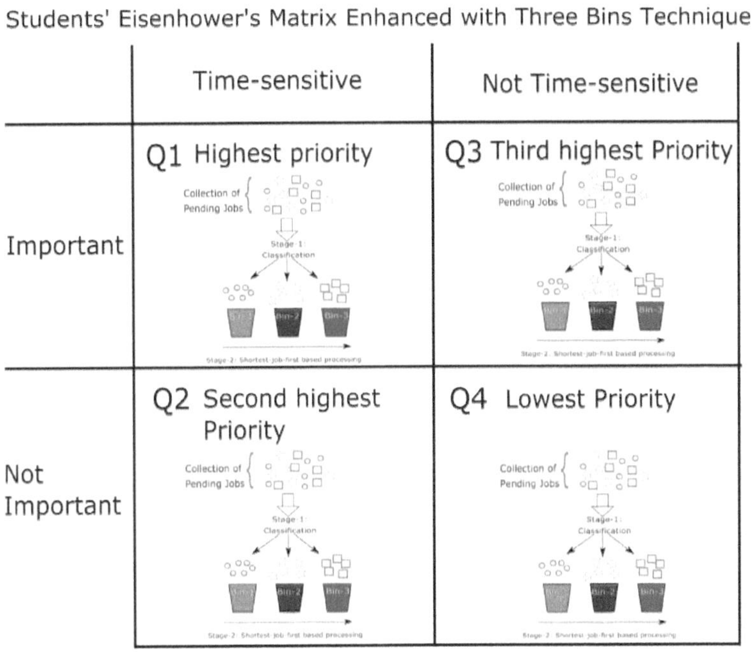

Figure 6.10: Using the Three Bins Technique in Students' Eisenhower's Matrix

6.7.6 Other Tools for Productivity Improvement

I suggest here a few tools that I use to improve general productivity in work as well as studies. I believe they will be useful for students as well as professionals. Some of the simple tools I use on a daily basis are: (i) Google Calendar, (ii) Checklist Diary, (iii) Idea Diary, and (iv) Timers.

Google Calendar [14] is a web-based calendar service offered by Google Inc. Google Calendar can be useful for scheduling or planning various activities. It is particularly suitable for scheduling recurring events or activities. For example, all the classes, labs, and other evaluation schedules can be managed very well using Google Calendar. Further, the calendar allows both desktop and email alerts. For academic scheduling, therefore, Google Calendar is a very useful tool.

Another useful tool that I suggest is a small diary, preferably a pocket diary that can be used as a *Checklist Diary*. The Checklist Diary can be used by a student to list items that are to be carried out. The list can be called either a *To Do list* or a *pending items list.* The items to be carried out during the day can be identified in order to cross them out at the end of the day. A quick review of the still pending matters can be conducted at any time of a day such that your daily efficiency or inefficiency can be evaluated. I found such a list improved my daily efficiency substantially.

One of the most fascinating tools that I use for my research and innovative ideas is *The Idea Diary*. The Idea Diary is a normal diary where I note down the ideas that I frequently get on various matters of my interest. Most interestingly, the ideas that are wild and innovative find place in such a diary. Regular or routine matters are not to be written in the diary. Each of the ideas can be briefly detailed with diagrams, description about operational methods, advantages, and disadvantages. Such a detailed description can be helpful for the user himself/herself in order to remember the key concept listed in the items of the diary. The Idea Diary is particularly useful for students because of the following reasons: (i) ideas originated by students are highly futuristic and as a result, it may take a long time before those ideas can be realized, (ii) ideas may be wild and not realizable at all, (iii) it may not be easy to convince others with one's ideas, (iv) writing the ideas down can help in avoiding negative criticisms that may arise when a student discusses his/her ideas with others, and (v) a student may realize some of his ideas later in his life when he is likely to have access to necessary resources for realizing the ideas. The Idea Diary is a very interesting tool for everyone, particularly for teachers and students.

Finally, timers or watches, that can be used to set alarms at certain repetitive intervals, can help a student in a significantly better way to review the progress made. Timers can be set to ring alarm at a specific time interval such as an hour, 30 minutes, or 15 minutes during your work. I often use one hour timers for low workload situations, 30 minutes timer in moderate workload situations, and 15 minutes timer during high workloads for efficient progress of work. When timer alarm rings, you can review the progress you made on the work. Such a timely feedback on the progress made can help motivate a student to complete more work in a time efficient manner.

Several tools such as Google Calendar, Checklist Diary, Idea Diary, and Timers, can be utilized by the teachers and students, in order to better progress on their productivity, efficiency, and usage of time.

6.8 Summary

This chapter discussed the teaching philosophies of various parts of the world that laid the foundation of modern education. My teaching philosophy is shaped by my teachers as well as my experience as a student and teacher. The key points in my teaching philosophy include the following: (i) teaching is a holy profession, (ii) feedback is inevitable for teaching, (iii) teaching is a mutual learning process, (iv) multi-modal teaching-learning process is natural. Further, a few tools such as Cornell note-taking method, Franklin's chart, Eisenhower's matrix, and the Three Bins technique, that are useful to teachers and students, were also discussed.

The philosophy of the school room in one generation will be the philosophy of government in the next.
- Abraham Lincoln.

Chapter 7
Conclusions

Those who educate children well are more to be honored than they who produce them; for these only gave them life, those the art of living well.
- Aristotle, Greek philosopher.

Multi-Track Modular Teaching (MT2) method helps in multi-modal learning of an academic course under teaching. MT2 accomplishes the multi-modal learning through the use of multiple parallel tracks defined within a course. Each track consists of an adaptive and customizable set of activity modules. A diversified set of tracks can provide all-round and deeper knowledge about the subject under study.

In Chapter 1, MT2 method is introduced and the questions such as When to use MT2 method and When not to use MT2 method were answered. MT2 method can be used in courses where the students are expected to develop deeper and all-round knowledge. Therefore, courses such as research-oriented courses, graduate study courses, and those requiring highest levels of skills can utilize MT2 method. In courses that are basic, general, and requiring no depth of learning, MT2 method is not suitable. Use of MT2 method requires highly talented teachers and teaching assistants as well.

Chapter 2 presented the details of MT2 method with various examples from the IIST Trivandrum, India, where the method was created, formalized, practiced, and revised. Examples from various real courses with three and four tracks were presented. Benefits of MT2 method were also highlighted.

Chapter 3 presented the considerations that need to be taken for designing tracks for an MT2 method based course. A large number of various possible tracks were provided for the benefit of the academicians. The type and nature of tracks shall be decided based on the following: (i) tracks shall follow the university's guidelines, (ii) tracks shall complement each other,(iii) tracks shall have minimal overlap, (iv) tracks shall be defined in unambiguous manner, (v) tracks shall be designed based on the instructor's plan for the course. Further, the number of tracks shall be determined based on (i) Essentiality of a track, (ii) Minimality of tracks, (iii) Clarity of tracks, and (iv) Complementarity of tracks. Each track shall be assigned appropriate credits based on the type of tracks as well as the effort involved in executing the activities of the track. Based on the inter-dependencies of the tracks' modules, tracks can be categorized as: (i) Synchronous, (ii) Semi-synchronous, and (iii) Asynchronous tracks.

Chapter 4 detailed the concept of modularity of activities defined as part of the tracks. Modularity of tracks helps in many ways: (i) Better understanding of the topics of the track, (ii) Adaptability and customization of the track, (iii) Simplifying the grading process, (iv) Making the tracks more interesting, and (v) Achieving better track synchronization. The choice of modules can be made for each track based on: (i) Synchrony of modules, (ii) Large Vs Small modules, and (iii) Many vs Small number of modules. Based on the difficulty level of the modules organized in sequence within a track, the modules can be considered as either (i) Constant difficulty Level modules, (ii) Progressive difficulty level modules, or (iii) Variable difficulty level modules. Many real-world examples of modules for various tracks were discussed in the chapter.

Chapter 5 presented the way in which MT2 method can be used to enhance Undergraduate Research (UGR) in universities. The four top ways of using MT2 in universities include: (i) Senior UG elective courses including the honor, minor, or specializations, (ii) Senior Design Project courses, (iii) Junior Elective courses, and (iv) selected Sophomore courses.

Chapter 6 presented the teaching philosophies from various regions of the world and the factors that shaped my teaching philosophy. Further, several productivity tools such as Cornell note-taking method, Franklin's chart, Eisenhower's matrix, and Three Bins technique were also presented for the benefit of teachers and students.

Do not train a child to learn by force or harshness; but direct them to it by what amuses their minds, so that you may be better able to discover with accuracy the peculiar bent of the genius of each.
- Plato (BC 427-BC 347) Greek philosopher.

Abbreviations

- ACM - Association of Computing Machinery
- AICTE - All India Council of Technical Education
- ASCI - Administrative Staff College of India
- CalIT2 - California Institute of Telecommunications and Information Technology
- CalSysNet - CalIT2 Systems and Networks Research Group
- DST - Department of Science and Technology
- DTR - Detailed Technical Review
- EECS - Electrical Engineering and Computer Science
- IEEE - Institute of Electrical and Electronics Engineers
- IIST - Indian Institute of Space science and Technology
- IITB - Indian Institute of Technology Bombay
- IITM - Indian Institute of Technology Madras
- IITs - Indian Institutes of Technology
- ITRA - Information Technology Research Academy
- IUSSTF - Indo-US Science and Technology Forum
- MHRD - Ministry of Human Resources Development
- MICRONet - Mobile Infrastructure for Coastal Region Offshore Communications and Networks
- MIT - Massachusetts Institute of Technology
- MOOC - Massive Open Online Course
- MRR - Mission Readiness Review
- MT2 - Multi-Track Modular Teaching
- NPTEL - National Program on Technology Enhanced Learning

- OBE - Outcome Based Evaluation
- PDR - Preliminary Design Review
- SDN - Software Defined Network
- TA - Teaching Assistant
- UCSD - University of California San Diego
- UG - Undergraduate
- UGR - Undergraduate Research
- WMN - Wireless Mesh Network

Acknowledgments

I alphabetically list and acknowledge my mentors, faculty colleagues, peer-researchers, academicians, expert professionals, and the Undergraduate, Masters, and Research students whose interactions helped me to understand and develop the idea of Multi-Track Modular Teaching (MT2) method and practice at IIST. For any inaccuracy in the list, I may please be pardoned.

- A Chandrasekar, Department of Earth and Space sciences, Indian Institute of Space science and Technology, Trivandrum, India.
- Abhishek Chakraborty, Department of Computer Science and Engineering, Indian Institute of Technology Madras, Chennai, 600036, India.
- Alexander Albert Stonier, Kongu Engineering College, Perundurai, Tamilnadu, India.
- Anjali Gulati, Isabella Thoburn College, Lucknow, India.
- Antony Franklin, Department of Computer Science and Engineering, Indian Institute of Technology Hyderabad, Hyderabad, Telengana, India.
- Anup S, Department of Aerospace, Indian Institute of Space science and Technology, Trivandrum, India.
- Anurag Kumar, Department of Electrical Communication Engineering, Indian Institute of Science, Bangalore, Karnataka, India.
- B. N. Suresh, Chancellor, Indian Institute of Space science and Technology, Trivandrum, India.
- Balaraman Ravindran, Department of Computer Science and Engineering, Indian Institute of Technology Madras, Chennai, Tamil Nadu, India.
- Bhaskar Rao, Department of Electrical and Computer Engineering, University of California San Diego, San Diego, CA, 92093, USA.
- Bheemarjuna Reddy Tamma, Department of Computer Science and Engineering, Indian Institute of Technology Hyderabad, Hyderabad, Telengana, India.
- Bindukumar Nair, State University of New York (SUNY) at Buffalo, New York, NY 14260, USA.
- C. R. Patil, R. C. Patel Institute of Pharmaceutical Education and Research, Shirpur, Maharashtra, India.

- C. Siva Ram Murthy, Department of Computer Science and Engineering, Indian Institute of Technology Madras, Chennai, Tamil Nadu, India.
- C.V. Anil Kumar, Department of Mathematics, Indian Institute of Space science and Technology, Thiruvananthapuram, Kerala, India.
- Chris Prema, Department of Avionics, Indian Institute of Space science and Technology, Thiruvananthapuram, Kerala, India.
- D. Manjunath, Department of Electrical Engineering, Indian Institute of Technology Bombay, Mumbai, Maharashtra, India.
- Debabrata Dalai, Department of Avionics, Indian Institute of Space science and Technology, Trivandrum, India.
- Deepak Mishra, Department of Avionics, Indian Institute of Space science and Technology, Thiruvananthapuram, Kerala, India.
- Deepak Thazhungal Govindan, Department of Mathematics, Indian Institute of Space Science and Technology, Thiruvananthapuram, Kerala, India.
- Dilip Krishnaswamy, Reliance Jio Infocomm Ltd, Bangalore, Karnataka, India.
- Divya R. S., Department of Avionics, Indian Institute of Space science and Technology, Trivandrum, India.
- Felix Bast, Central University of Punjab, Bathinda, India.
- Hema A. Murthy, Department of Computer Science and Engineering, Indian Institute of Technology Madras, Chennai, Tamil Nadu, India.
- Joseph Kuruvilla, Department of Chemistry, Indian Institute of Space science and Technology, Trivandrum, India.
- K. R. Ramakrishnan, Department of Electrical Engineering, Indian Institute of Science, Bengaluru, Karnataka, India.
- K. Sivan, Chairman, Indian Space Research Organization, Bangalore, India.
- K. Venkata Krishnan, ISRO Head Quarters, Bangalore, India.
- Kurien Issac, Department of Aerospace, Indian Institute of Space science and Technology, Trivandrum, India.
- M. V. Dhekane, Department of Avionics, Indian Institute of Space science and Technology, Trivandrum, India.
- Madhavan P Nair, Department of Immunology and Nano-Medicine, Florida International University, Miami, FL 33199, USA.
- Manoj T. Nair, Department of Aerospace, Indian Institute of Space science and Technology, Trivandrum, India.

- Massimo Franceschetti, Department of Electrical and Computer Engineering, University of California San Diego, San Diego, CA 92093, USA.
- Mohan. G., Administrative Staff College of India, Hyderabad, India.
- Mohan Trivedi, Department of Electrical and Computer Engineering, University of California San Diego, San Diego, CA 92093, USA.
- N. S. Rajput, Indian Institute of Technology (BHU), India.
- Nalini Venkatasubramanian, Department of Computer Science, University of California Irvine, Irvine, CA, USA.
- Narendra Ahuja, Information Technology Research Academy, New Delhi, India.
- Neeraj Mishra, Indian Institute of Technology, Kanpur, India.
- O. S. K. S. Sastri, Central University of Himachal Pradesh, Dharamshala, India.
- P. C. Narayan, Indian Institute of Management, Bangalore, India.
- P. D. Jose, Indian Institute of Management, Bangalore, India.
- Pamela Cosman, Department of Electrical and Computer Engineering, University of California San Diego, San Diego, CA 92093, USA.
- Pradeep Yammiyavar, Indian Institute of Technology Guwahati, India.
- Prakash Javadekar, Cabinet Minister, Government of India, New Delhi, India.
- Priscilla Koshy, Department of Avionics, Indian Institute of Space science and Technology, Trivandrum, India.
- Priyadarshnam Hari, Department of Avionics, Indian Institute of Space science and Technology, Thiruvananthapuram, Kerala, India.
- R. Parvathi, Vellalar College for Women, Erode, Tamilnadu, India.
- R. Umamaheswaran, Scientific Secretary, Indian Space Research Organization, Bangalore, India.
- Rajarathnam Chandramouli, Department of Electrical and Computer Engineering, Stevens Institute of Technology, Hoboken, NJ, USA.
- Rajesh Gupta, Department of Computer Science and Engineering, University of California San Diego, San Diego, CA 92093, USA.
- Rajiv Misra, Indian Institute of Technology Patna, Patna, India.
- Raju George, Department of Mathematics, Indian Institute of Space science and Technology, Trivandrum, India.

- Ramesh R. Rao, Department of Electrical and Computer Engineering, University of California San Diego, San Diego, CA 92093, USA.
- Ramya Ranganathan, Indian Institute of Management, Bangalore, India.
- S. Balamurugan, Amrita School of Engineering, Coimbatore, India.
- Sam Zachariah, Department of Avionics, Indian Institute of Space science and Technology, Trivandrum, India.
- Sarath Babu, Department of Avionics, Indian Institute of Space science and Technology, Trivandrum, India.
- Selvaganesan Narayanasamy, Department of Avionics, Indian Institute of Space science and Technology, Thiruvananthapuram, Kerala, India.
- Sharad Mehrotra, School of Information and Computer Science, University of California Irvine, Irvine, California, USA.
- Sheeba Rani J., Department of Avionics, Indian Institute of Space science and Technology, Thiruvananthapuram, Kerala, India.
- Sujit Dey, Department of Electrical and Computer Engineering, University of California San Diego, San Diego, CA 92093, USA.
- T. V. Prabhakar, Indian Institute of Technology, Kanpur, India.
- Tara Javidi, Department of Electrical and Computer Engineering, University of California San Diego, San Diego, CA 92093, USA.
- Uday B. Desai, Department of Electrical Engineering, Indian Institute of Technology Hyderabad, Hyderabad, Telengana, India.
- Venkataramana Badarla, Indian Institute of Technology Tirupati, Tirupati, Andhra Pradesh, India.
- Venkatesh T., Indian Institute of Technology Guwahati, North Guwahati, Assam, India.
- Vinay Kumar Dadhwal, Director, Indian Institute of Space science and Technology, Trivandrum, 695547, India.
- Vinay Joseph Ribeiro, Indian Institute of Technology Delhi, New Delhi, India.
- Vineeth B. S., Department of Avionics, Indian Institute of Space science and Technology, Thiruvananthapuram, Kerala, India.
- Y. V. N. Krishnamurthy, Indian Institute of Space science and Technology, Trivandrum, India.

I would additionally like to acknowledge my students who took the Wireless Mesh Networks or Computer Networks courses over the years at IIST Trivandrum where I developed MT2 method. Here is the list of students that I acknowledge. Any omissions in this list are regretted.

- A. Navya Sree
- Aaditya Sarda
- Aarathi Ramesh Muppalla
- Abhee Parekh
- Abhinav Paul
- Abhishek Bhaumick
- Ajay Salas
- Ajit R Kanale
- Akella Sesha Sai
- AmalKrishna R
- Amit Kumar
- Amit Kumar Upadhyay
- Anchal Yadav
- Anirban Paul
- Ankur Verma
- Annadi Vivek Reddy
- Annam Madhulika
- Ansuman Palo
- Anugolu Purnesh Sai Ram
- Anurag Shukla
- Archana C. M.
- Archit Khanduja
- Arkarup Gupta
- Arnab Karmakar
- Arun K. P.
- Arushi Seth
- Arvind Vairavan
- Awadhesh Kumar Maurya
- Aziya Nizin P
- Battula Greeshma
- Betha Shirisha
- Boyapati Ujjwala
- Bylapudi Prasanna Kumar
- Chaitavya Bhardwaj
- Chandan Kumar
- Chinmoy Matre
- Chinmoy S Mathre
- Chudasama Yuvrajsinh Surendrakumar

- Datar Kaustubh Kiran
- Debajyoti Chakrabarti
- Deeconda Dheeraj
- Deepak Kumar
- Devasani Bharat
- Devendra Singh
- Devireddy Pramod Reddy
- Digvijay Pandey
- Divyang Arora
- Duvvuru Tharunteja
- Eda Solman Rupesh
- Egala Ugesh
- Evani Anupam Sarma
- Gade Sree Ram
- Gandikota Rohit
- Gargi Sunil
- Gaurav Jain
- Gubbala Kiran
- Gudey Meghanath
- Gulshan Gupta
- Harmeet Singh
- Himanshu Saini
- Ishan Chaturvedi
- Ishika Ghara
- Ishita Ganjoo
- Ivan Joseph Roy
- Janga Sai Rama Krishna
- Jaya Krishna M
- Jeldi Kamal Kumar
- Jiljo K. Moncy
- Jitendra Kumar Dayama
- K.M. Deepshikha
- Kakumanu Sai Ram
- Kalpita Mandal
- Kamma Naga Praneeth
- Kaninika Pant
- Karan
- Karri V. R. Dinesh Kumar Reddy

- Karthick M
- Karumuru Venkata Niranjan Sai
- Keshav Dayal
- Khushnandan Rai
- Konatham Samuel
- Kondam Vamshi Krishna
- Konganapalle Gowthami
- Kosuru Sai Malleswar
- Kota Sandeep
- Kotagiri Srilekha
- Kumari Pooja
- Kunal Choudhary
- Lendegaonkar Deepak
- Lijo P. Jose
- Madhura Bhanu Teja
- Makkuva Shyam Vinay
- Malai Devan P
- Malreddy Yashwanth Reddy
- Mamidi Aditya Vamsi
- Manasa N. K.
- Manasvi G
- Manigilla Haindavi
- Manohar Katam
- Manoj Kumar
- Mantena Dileep Varma
- Meher Jain
- Menpara Neel Mukeshbhai
- Mithun P. V.
- Mohak Varshneya
- Mohammad Rameez Khasim
- Mohit Kumar Soni
- Muna Kumar Singh
- Mynam Harinath
- N Anand
- Nagakusuma Dupam
- Neelam J. S. S. V. Prasad
- Neha Kumari
- Nikky Srivastava

- Nirmal Kumar
- Nisha George
- Nitin Rai
- Nitish Kumar
- Nivedita Gaur
- Om Siddharth Krishna T
- Pabolu Viswambhara
- Palash Joshi
- Pamidiparthi Ravi Teja Naidu
- Pankaj Toppo
- Paul Antony
- Pera Pogu Ravi Teja
- Polsani Kaushik Rao
- Pothuri Ram Sukumar
- Potluri Vamsi Krishna
- Prabodh Shreedhar Katti
- Pragallapati Srikanth
- Pragya Shah
- Prakhar Gupta
- Prashant Ranjan
- Pratabidya Panda
- Prathaviraj Meena
- Pratik Wankhede
- Pratyush Prasun Das
- Priti Singh
- Priyanka Rathod
- Rahul Sekhar R
- Rajat Attri
- Rajesh Azmera
- Rajesh Muntha
- Rajnish Kumar Yadav
- Rallabhandi Sreedhar
- Ramesh Banoth
- Rashmi
- Ratakonda Anirudh
- Ravi Kumar
- Reuben Chacko Thomas
- Rohit T. Kurian

- Rohit Tyagi
- Sachin Garg
- Sagnik Dutta
- Saket Chawla
- Samvram Sahu
- Sanjay Kumar
- Sanjutha Indrajit
- Sanket Patel
- Sarode Anuj Ghanshyambhai
- Satyaduth Medapati
- Shashi Krishna
- Shikha Maharana
- Shinde Sayali Deepak
- Shishir Kumar S. Chandra
- Shivam Arora
- Shravan Kumar
- Shubham Chauhan
- Shubhankar Biswas
- Siddharth Srivastava
- Singamaneni Anusha
- Sircilla Anusha
- Sneha Gem Mathew
- Soma Sinha
- Somarouthu Sai Srinivas
- Sougata Nag
- Sourajit Debnath
- Sourav Maji
- Sreekakulam Venkata Tharun
- Srinika Selvam
- Subashsundar N
- Subhajit Majumder
- Sukirna Roy
- Suragala Kiran Kumar
- Suraj Kumar
- Suraj R
- Susmitha Suresh
- Suvransu Sekhar Patra
- T. Harshaveena

- Tuhin Paul
- V. Adithya Krishnan
- Vaddadi Sree Vamsi
- Vamshi Tirupati Bollam
- Varun Kumar K
- Venkata Pujitha Bhavanasi
- Vinay Gajmoti
- Vineeth Kumar Kota
- Vinod P
- Vivek Dholpuria
- Yarramsetty Naga Rahul
- Yawatkar Shakun Rajan
- Yogesh Parth

Author's Biography

B. S. Manoj is currently Professor and Head, Department of Avionics, Indian Institute of Space science and Technology (IIST), Thiruvananthapuram, India. He worked as Associate Professor at IIST from 2011-2016 at the Department of Avionics, IIST.

He was an Infosys doctoral student during 2000 - 2003 in the Department of Computer Science and Engineering at the Indian Institute of Technology Madras, Chennai, India, where he focused on the development of architectures and protocols for Ad hoc wireless networks and next generation hybrid wireless network architectures. He received his PhD degree in Computer Science and Engineering from IIT Madras in 2004. He completed his M.Tech ECE degree with 2nd rank from Pondicherry Engineering College, Pondicherry Central University, Pondicherry, India, in 1998.

He has worked as a Senior Engineer with Banyan Networks Pvt. Ltd., Chennai, India from 1998 to 2000 where his primary responsibility included design and development of protocols for real-time traffic support in data networks. During January 2004 - January 2005, he was a Project Officer at IIT, Madras, India. From January 2005 to January 2011, he was at the University of California San Diego, San Diego, USA, working initially as a post-doctoral researcher and later as an assistant research scientist and lecturer.

He co-authored two text books titled: (i) "Complex Networks: A Networking and Signal Processing Perspective," published by Pearson, New York, February 2018 and (ii) "Ad hoc Wireless Networks: Architectures and Protocols," published by Prentice Hall PTR, New Jersey, NJ, USA in May 2004. He is a recipient of the following honors/awards: (i) Teaching Innovator 2016 certificate from Ministry of Human Resource Development, Government of India, for developing Multi-Track Modular-Teaching method, (ii) co-authored the paper titled "Graph Fourier Transform Based on Directed Laplacian" co-authored with Rahul Singh and Abhishek Chakraborty that was awarded Springer Best Student Paper

Award at the 11th International Conference on Signal Processing and Communications (SPCOM) 2016, Indian Institute of Science (IISc) Bangalore, India, June 2016, (iii) IEEE ICNC 2015 Outstanding Leadership Award, (iv) Co-authored the paper titled "Comparative evaluation of ARIMA and ANFIS for modeling of wireless network traffic time series," published in Springer/EURASIP Journal on Wireless Communications and Networking in January 2014, which was recognized as highly accessed by the journal, (v) Recipient of the Elsevier Ad hoc Networks Journal's Top Cited Article during 2005-2010 Award for the article titled "Quality of Service Provisioning in Ad Hoc Wireless Networks: A Survey of Issues and Solutions," co-authored with T. B. Reddy, I. Karthigeyan, and C. Siva Ram Murthy and published in Elsevier Ad Hoc networks, Vol. 4, Issue 1, 2006, (vi) Recipient of the Best Paper Award for the paper entitled "On Optimizing Non-Asymptotic Throughput of Wireless Mesh Networks" co-authored with P. Zhou and Ramesh Rao, at the 5th Annual IEEE Consumer Communications and Networking Conference 2008 (IEEE CCNC 2008) held in Las Vegas, USA, during January 10-12, 2008, (vii) Recipient of IBM Outstanding PhD Student/Thesis Award for the year 2004, (viii) recipient of ISCA (Indian Science Congress Association) Young Scientist Award for the year 2003, (ix) Recipient of the Best Paper Award for the paper entitled "A Novel Battery Aware MAC Protocol for Ad hoc Wireless Networks," co-authored with S. Jayashree and C. Siva Ram Murthy, at the 11th International Conference on High Performance Computing 2004 (HiPC 2004) held in Bangalore, India during December 19-22, 2004, (x) Recipient of the Best Paper Award for the paper entitled "Multi-hop Cellular Networks: Architecture and Protocols for Best-effort and Real time Communication," co-authored with R. Ananthapadmanabha and C. Siva Ram Murthy, at the First Inter Research Institute Student Seminar in Computer Science 2002 (IRISS 2002) held at the Indian Institute of Science, Bangalore, India, during March 28-29, 2002.

His research interests include Complex Networks, Cyber Security, Cognitive Networks, Ad hoc wireless networks, wireless mesh networks, software defined networks, delay tolerant networks, and wireless sensor networks.

मानव संसाधन विकास मंत्रालय
MINISTRY OF HUMAN RESOURCE DEVELOPMENT

पंडित मदन मालवीय राष्ट्रीय शिक्षक एवं शिक्षण मिशन
Pandit Madan Mohan Malaviya
National Mission on Teachers and Teaching

एडमिनिस्ट्रेटिव स्टाफ कॉलेज ऑफ इंडिया, हैदराबाद
Administrative Staff College of India, Hyderabad.

शिक्षण अन्वेषक पुरस्कार 2016
TEACHING INNOVATOR AWARD 2016

प्रशंसा प्रमाण पत्र

प्रो बी एस मनोज, भारतीय अंतरिक्ष विज्ञान और प्रौद्योगिकी संस्थान को उच्चतर शिक्षा में शिक्षण पद्धति के क्षेत्र में उनके द्वारा किये गए नवोन्मेष की सराहना करते हुए शिक्षण अन्वेषक 2016 के रूप में यह प्रशंसा पत्र प्रदान किया जाता है।

Certificate of Appreciation

is awarded to

Prof B S Manoj *of Indian Institute of Space Science and Technology as a* **Teaching Innovator - 2016** *in higher education and his innovation in the area of* **Teaching Method**.

(जी मोहन)
समन्वयक, पंमगोमाराशिमिटीटी
(G. MOHAN)
Coordinator, PMMMNMTT

(आर सुब्रह्मण्यम)
सचिव उ.शि. भारत सरकार
(R. SUBRAHMANYAM)
Secretary, HE, Government of India

4 January, 2019

Figure A: Recognition certificate received by the author from the Ministry of Human Resources Development (MHRD), Government of India, for developing Multi-Track Modular Teaching (MT2) method.

Figure B: Dr. B. S. Manoj (second from right) receives the appreciation certificate from the then Honorable Minister Shri. Prakash Javadekar (third from right), Ministry of Human Resources Development (MHRD), Government of India, for developing the Multi-Track Modular Teaching (MT2) method at a function held on 4th January 2019, New Delhi, India. [Photograph courtesy: Prof. G. Mohan, Professor, Administrative Staff College of India, Hyderabad, India.]

Other books co-authored by Dr. B. S. Manoj, available through Amazon.com are listed here:

C. Siva Ram Murthy and B. S. Manoj, **Ad hoc Wireless Networks: Architectures and Protocols**, Prentice Hall PTR, New Jersey, May 2004.

B. S. Manoj, Abhishek Chakraborty, and Rahul Singh, ***Complex Networks: A Networking and Signal Processing Perspective****, Pearson, New York, February 2018.*

Notes

Chapter 1 — Introduction

[1]The UC San Diego Division of California Institute of Telecommunications and Information Technology (CalIT2) was recently renamed as Qualcomm Institute (QI). The website of the institute can be found at: http://qi.ucsd.edu/.

[2]The original website: http://calsysnet.calit2.net/Indo-US/

Chapter 2 — The Method

Chapter 3 — The Tracks

[1]The word complementarity is a noun form related to the word complementary with meaning *adding something in a way that enhances or improves* or *mutually supplying each other's lack.*

Chapter 4 — The Modularity

[1]One example of Gifted and Talented Education (GATE) System where practice of flexible student-paced education approach attempted is at the San Diego Unified School District of California, USA. Website: https://www.sandiegounified.org

[2]A node in that course is a wireless mesh network (WMN) router that is created out of an embedded computer with wireless interfaces that can provide multi-hop wireless network operation. Each student team built one WMN node before proceeding with the network experiment modules.

Chapter 5 — MT2 Method and UG Research

[1]Sophomore refers to the second year students of a four year degree program.

Chapter 6 — Teaching Philosophies and Productivity Tools

[1]Elon Reeve Musk is a visionary who plays various illustrious roles including the following: a high caliber engineer, a pioneering technology entrepreneur, billionaire investor, founder and CEO of SpaceX, co-founder and CEO of Tesla, Inc, founder of The Boring Company, co-founder and CEO of Neuralink, co-founder and co-chairman of OpenAI, and co-founder of PayPal. He is credited with many technological innovations and disruptive business practices that his peer technocrats could not accomplish.

[2]Guru is a Sanskrit word for a highly revered teacher who dispels darkness of knowledge and brings a student closer to the light of knowledge. The word Guruis used from ancient to modern India as well as certain other parts of the world. In current day India, Guru refers to a person who is a mentor, master, spiritual leader, guiding source, and even respected people with non-teaching mentoring roles.

[3]Exact accounts of Plato's birth and life times are not known. This is an approximate of his life time as known to historians.

Chapter 7 — Conclusions

Appendix: Catalogue for AV 484 Wireless Mesh Networks

Title of the course: ***Wireless Mesh Networks***

Course No: ***AV 484***

Audience: ***Senior undergrads and Graduate students***

Units/Credit: ***3***

Prerequisites: ***AV 321 or Consent of Instructor***

Tentative Catalog Syllabus:

Introduction and overview of Wireless Mesh Networks, Evolution of Wireless Mesh Networks, Architectural issues in Wireless Mesh Networks, Capacity of Wireless Mesh Networks, Layer-wise Protocol design issues in Wireless Mesh Networks, MAC layer protocols for Wireless Mesh Networks, Network layer protocols for Wireless Mesh Networks, Transport layer protocols for Wireless Mesh Networks, Load Balancing in Wireless Mesh Networks, Wide Area Wireless Mesh Networks, Design issues for Wide Area Wireless Mesh Networks, Resource allocation problems in Wireless Mesh Networks, Hybrid wireless mesh networks including WiMAX networks, and Layer-wise open research problems on protocol design for Wireless Mesh Networks.

References

1. Yan Zhang, Jijun Luo, and Honglin Hu, *Wireless Mesh Networking: Architectures, Protocols and Standards,* Auerbach Publications, December 2006.
2. Ian Akyildiz and Xudong Wang, *Wireless Mesh Networks,* John Wiley and Sons, March 2009.
3. Sudip Misra, Subhas Chandra Misra, Isaac Woungang, *Guide to Wireless Mesh Networks,* Springer, December 2010.
4. C. Siva Ram Murthy and B. S. Manoj, *Ad hoc Wireless Networks: Architectures and Protocols,* Prentice Hall PTR, New Jersey, May 2004.

Bibliography

[1] "ACM digital library". https://dl.acm.org/. Accessed: 2019-03-25.

[2] "Administrative Staff College of India". https://www.asci.org.in. Accessed: 2018-10-17.

[3] "All India Council of Technical Education". https://www.aicte-_india.org/. Accessed: 2019-03-30.

[4] "CalIT2 Systems and Networks Research Group". http://calsysnet.calit2.net/. Accessed: 2018-10-17.

[5] "CommView: A powerful network monitor and analyzer". https://www.tamos.com/products/commwifi/. Accessed: 2018-12-02.

[6] "Coursera: A MOOC Service Provider". https://www.coursera.org/. Accessed: 2019-03-30.

[7] "Dr. Dharmaraja's Website". http://web.iitd.ac.in/~dharmar/. Accessed: 2018-10-17.

[8] "Dr. T. B. Reddy's Home page". https://www.iith.ac.in/~tbr/. Accessed: 2018-10-17.

[9] "Dr. V. K. Dadhwal's Linkedin Profile page". https://www.linkedin.com/in/vinaykdadhwal/?originalSubdomain=in. Accessed: 2018-10-17.

[10] "Dwight D. Eisenhower". https://en.wikipedia.org/wiki/Dwight_D._Eisenhower. Accessed: 2019-03-25.

[11] "EdX: A MOOC Service Provider". https://www.edx.org/. Accessed: 2019-03-30.

[12] "Elsevier, Inc.". https://www.elsevier.com/. Accessed: 2019-03-25.

[13] "Estimated class sizes of more than 90 national universities.". http://publicuniversityhonors.com/2015/10/20/estimated-_class-_sizes-_more-_than-_90-_national-_universities/. Accessed: 2019-01-27.

[14] "Google Calendar". https://www.google.com/calendar. Accessed: 2019-03-25.

[15] "Home page of Dr. V. S. Ramachandran". http://cbc.ucsd.edu/ramabio.html. Accessed: 2019-04-08.

[16] "IEEExplore Digital Library". https://ieeexplore.ieee.org/Xplore/home.jsp. Accessed: 2019-03-25.

[17] "Indian Institute of Space Science and Technology". https://www.iist.ac.in/. Accessed: 2018-10-17.

[18] "Indo-US Science and Technology Forum". https://www.iusstf.org/. Accessed: 2018-10-17.

[19] "Indo-US Summer School on Systems and Networks". http://calsysnet.calit2.net/Indo-_US/. Accessed: 2018-10-17.

[20] "Information Technology Research Academy". https://itra.medialabasia.in/. Accessed: 2019-04-24.

[21] "Jupyter Notebook: An Interactive Computational Environment". https://ipython.org/notebook.html/. Accessed: 2018-12-02.

[22] "Matlab: A multi-paradigm numerical computing environment". https://www.mathworks.com/products/matlab.html/. Accessed: 2018-12-02.

[23] "National Program on Technology Enhanced Learning". https://onlinecourses.nptel.ac.in/. Accessed: 2019-03-30.

[24] "NetSim: A network simulator and emulator software". https://www.tetcos.com/. Accessed: 2018-12-02.

[25] "Network Animator". https://www.isi.edu/nsnam/nam/. Accessed: 2018-12-02.

[26] "Network Simulator-2". https://www.isi.edu/nsnam/ns/. Accessed: 2018-12-02.

[27] "Neuralink". https://www.neuralink.com/. Accessed: 2019-4-09.

[28] "OPNET: A Network Simulator Platform". https://www.riverbed.com/in/products/steelcentral/opnet.html/. Accessed: 2018-12-02.

[29] "Qualnet: A Network Simulator Software". https://web.scalable-_networks.com/qualnet-_network-_simulator-_software. Accessed: 2018-12-02.

[30] "Springer, Inc.". https://www.springer.com/gp. Accessed: 2019-03-25.

[31] "Swayam Prabha Self-learning Program of Government of India". https://swayam.gov.in/. Accessed: 2019-03-30.

[32] "Tactile Internet". https://www.itu.int/en/ITU-_T/techwatch/Pages/tactile-_internet.aspx. Accessed: 2019-04-09.

[33] "Udacity: A MOOC Service Provider". https://in.udacity.com/. Accessed: 2019-03-30.

[34] "UDTNsim: Urban Delay Tolerant Network Simulator". https://github.com/iist-_sysnet/UDTNSim/. Accessed: 2018-12-02.

[35] "Wireshark Network Protocol Analyzer". https://www.wireshark.org/. Accessed: 2018-12-02.

[36] Benjamin Franklin. *The Autobiography of Benjamin Franklin*. G. P. Putnam's Sons, New York and London, 1889.

Index

www.ingramcontent.com/pod-product-compliance
Lightning Source LLC
Chambersburg PA
CBHW022147160726
48282CB00024B/216
9789353615826